"...Your writing is so kitchen table."

at the

    -Shari McMinn
    Homeschooler
    Author, Editor

"...I love this book, having a hard time putting it down."
    -Stephanie Malcom, Author,
    Blogger at stephanieamalcome.com,
    Homemaker, and mom of six kids

"...easy to read and some really great ideas!"
    -Sandra K.

"The introduction grabbed my attention and I kept finding myself saying, yes, yes, and YES!"
    -Heather Lasher, Homeschooling mom of seven kids

"Just read Chapter One and I'm already thankful you've written this. I am VERY much a practical, give me instructions to follow, type of person...and this is doing it for me! It's not too rigid. It's more like...here are some ways to fit this in where you already are in life."
    -Tonya Hankins, Homeschooling mom of eight

"I was so excited to get my hands on Amber's book. As a homeschooling mom of 11 kiddos, I am ALWAYS looking to glean great insight from other moms who have been there and done that! That's Amber. My ultimate favorite thing about this book is Amber's values on priorities and the power we all have as moms. We're always examples to our kids. Amber's book helps you work through all the thoughts, feelings, and practical parts of being a homeschooling mama so that you can be the best example you can be! I highly recommend this book to any mom, no matter where you're in your homeschooling journey!"
    -Jill Martin, Coach at Martin Faith & Fitness,
    Community Leader at Strong Hearts, Strong Women,
    and Homeschooling mom of 11 kids

"...written in an approachable, yet applicable format..."
    -Cassie Kitzmiller, Homeschooling mom, Blogger at
    Findingbeautyintheeveryday.

"I've been homeschooling and homemaking for a decade. I've 'been there, done that,' and found systems I love and some I'm not so fond of. And yet, I found a treasure chest at my fingertips when I opened Amber's book. She's taken all the wisdom and encouragement that homeschooling moms could ever need and compiled it into one volume. Amber talks about nurturing our own relationship with God, keeping our marriage where it belongs, routines for homeschooling, running a home and more. This is THE Go-To book for homeschooling mamas who really do want to do 'it all' without being burdened by overwhelm and just need someone to show them how to make it work. This is going to be my new gift for homeschool mom friends, and a book I highlight, make notes in, and someday pass on to my daughter.

-Lisa Yvonne, blogger at gracefulabandon.com
And homeschooling mom of eight kids

Occasionally a book comes along and while reading it I'm thinking the whole time, "Where was this book when I need it?" This is one of those books.

-Deb Shelly, Retired veteran homeschool mom of 20 years

I LOVE this book! It's an easy read and I especially enjoy the stories. They really connect me to the author and what she's trying to convey. I feel like The Homeschooling Housewife was written for me so that I can be the wife and mother that God has called me to be!

-Stephanie Donahue, Blogger at aromamama.com and homeschooling mom of three kids

"I feel like Amber is sitting here talking to me over coffee and sharing her life with me. So much of what she talks about resonates with me - so many things touched on that I've been thinking about and trying to figure out along my journey as a homeschool mom of five young kids. I so appreciate Amber sharing the wisdom from her years of experience and the godly advice and guidance that's so applicable to every area of life!"

-Beth Love, homeschooling mom of five kids

"I am loving every aspect of your book. It speaks directly to where I am at! So far, my favorite section is the practical ways to share your faith with your kids! I love the ideas of telling them great mission stories!" **Amber M**

The Homeschooling Housewife

Juggling It ALL, One Priority at a Time

Amber Fox

Copyright

"You're as much serving God in looking after your own children, training them up in God's fear, minding the house, and making your household a church for God as you would be if you had been called to lead an army in battle for the Lord of Hosts."

~ Charles Spurgeon

Acknowledgements

There are certain things that could never be accomplished without the help of a team. It took a team to realize, *The Homeschooling Housewife*, and I'm blessed with some of the best!

The head of my team is my ever-faithful and sweet, sweet, husband. Ben, without you, this book would never have happened. You encouraged me through one of the most challenging tasks I have ever undertaken and reminded me that my mission was first for God. You told me I could write a book when I wasn't really sure I could, and you believed I would do it! You complete me; therefore this book is just as much yours as it is mine.

Thank you for the meals you cooked, the responsibilities you shouldered while I was writing, for endlessly entertaining the kids, (and flying baby Micah to me for nursing sessions while writing), the endless hours of formatting and reformatting when I changed my mind on styling, and most importantly, the Christ-like example you are to the kids and me every day. Through your love and provision, you have made being "The Homeschooling Housewife" my favorite job in the world. I absolutely adore you! You're the love of my life!

To my kids:

Logan, Lydia, Carter, Jake, Nadia, Nick, and baby Micah, you are all the realization of a dream. Since I was a little girl, I only ever wanted to be a wife and a mommy. You all make my job so fun and incredible. The love I feel for each one you can't be put into words. Staying home with you and having the privilege of teaching each of you is one of the most fulfilling things I could ever imagine doing.

I thoroughly enjoy spending every day with all of you! Thank you for being so patient with me while I wrote this book. The days got long, but, Jake, your 'icy' ice-waters got me through! The smiles on each of your faces and the long hugs and words of encouragement kept me going! I love you all!

To my parents:

Thank you for raising me to seek after a godly husband! I'm eternally grateful you raised me to love God and look for a husband who did as well. Your encouragement has meant the world to me.

Mom, thank you for telling me years ago that you thought I should write a book. Your voice rang in my head as I was writing, and I knew that if you thought I could do it, I could!

Dad, you taught me the gift of reading, which eventually transformed into the gift of writing. I remember our Saturday morning trips to the library when we would read all the fun books together! I don't think either of us ever thought it would turn me into an author!

I love you both!

To my Grandma:

Thank you for all the time you spent teaching me the rules of etiquette and hospitality. I've always held onto the memories of setting the table special and fancy. I remember you telling me that one day I'd need to know those rules to serve in my own house. Thank you for helping me carry on the tradition of love and hospitality. You gave me a love for homemaking long before I ever had a family. I'll never forget all the talks we've had in your kitchen as I sat at the breakfast nook and chattered away, dreaming of my own family somewhere way off in the future! I love you!

To Stacey:

My "Iron Sharpens Iron" friend. I can't even begin to express all that your friendship means to me. You've laughed and cried beside me and encouraged me along the way. Thank you for the love you've shown and the help you've given, and, by the way, you're an awesome launch team coordinator! I love you!

To Stephanie:

When you said, "Amber, you should write a book," I thought, "Yeah, right!" Yet, here it's! Without your encouragement and our afternoon Facetime chats, this book wouldn't be! Thank you for encouraging me to write what was on my heart. I hope you're blessed by it!

To my Editors:

Meg, may God bless your beautiful heart! Your ability to polish and refine my book means more to me than you'll ever know. God has used your gift of editing to bring this book to completion. Thank you for your hard work and energy dedicated to refining what I could not. I appreciate you!

And a special thank you to Grace E. I appreciate your hard work and diligence. You have a gift!

To my Photographer, Brian S. of Sawbridge Studio:

You're simply amazing! When you first posed the idea of putting me on the cover of my own book, I couldn't even imagine how, yet you created everything I hoped for and then some! Thank you for your endless hours of editing until we got it "just right." You made this such a fun project! It turned out *exactly* how I imagined it. Oh, and I had the most fun time letting everyone know that I had an up and coming photo shoot for my new book!

To My Homeschooling Housewife Launch Team:

You guys are the best! You made launching a book fun and exciting! Your encouragement and help has been a treasure! I'm grateful for each and every one of you!

And to Jesus, My Lord and Savior:

Thank you for saving me and filling me with your grace and righteousness. Without you, I am nothing. It's my pleasure to serve you by serving my family.

Table of contents

Introduction

As a homeschooling mom, you have a lot on your plate, as in a TON! Some days, you may feel like you're scrambling to keep up with basic human needs. I'm sure there are times when you don't know where to even start with everything that's thrown at you.

The kids are staring at you with hungry eyes *again*, and dishes are piled high in the sink, leftover from last night's meal. You haven't gotten dressed yet, since you forgot to put the clothes in the dryer before you turned in last night because you were rushing up the stairs to nurse your screaming baby, not to mention the pile of papers that needs to be graded, and your struggling reader keeps looking at you with tears in her eyes because she needs more help. You feel pulled in a million different directions, yet there's only one of you to go around.

The Homeschooling Housewife has been designed to help you know *exactly* how to start balancing your priorities, and it's easier than you thought. Discovering how to juggle your responsibilities is simple; you just need to know how to identify and then align everything on your plate. I'll walk you through how to manage your priorities, so you'll be left without a doubt. You'll have things under better control and will be able to juggle it all, one priority at a time.

This book is for people like you who don't know how to balance everything, people who love their families and want to serve them joyfully but find themselves struggling to keep up. *The Homeschooling Housewife* has been designed to help you feel more at peace and less like you're about to lose your mind. After reading it, you'll feel in control and be able to handle multiple demands, all with an attitude of dignity and grace.

I get it! I am a homeschooling, stay-at-home wife and mom of seven kiddos. Since I've been teaching my kids at home for more than twelve years, I've been right where you are. Over the years, I've gone through periods of time where I felt like I had no idea how I could handle it all. It's taken me up to this point to realize I can't, and I'm about to share with you all the tips that have made me succeed at homeschooling while juggling all the responsibilities that come with being a wife and mom.

I know what it's like to realize I forgot to defrost the meat *again* half an hour before we should be eating; the library books are overdue; my seventh grader is struggling with science, and I meant to spend one-on-one time with my middle child, but I just never got the chance. Being a homeschooling mom means there are usually more responsibilities than enough of you to go around. You can't meet every need one-hundred percent of the time and you need to give yourself grace. *The Homeschooling Housewife* will help you find a balance between all your priorities.

I've talked to hundreds of homeschooling moms like you and gathered information to see if my struggles were as common as I thought. The answer was a resounding YES! Now, more than ever, homeschooling moms just like you feel like they can't juggle everything they have on their plates.

This isn't a book about *finding* your priorities - you already have a ton. This book will encourage you to manage the priorities you *already have*. The best part about *The Homeschooling Housewife* is that, as you read it, you'll improve your juggling skills right from the very beginning as we examine each priority together, one at a time. As you learn to juggle each one well, you'll see that adding another priority is a breeze. Starting with the first chapter, you can begin gaining control today.

This book is jam-packed with actionable points that will help you organize parts of your life and make you feel like you have a better handle on the things that are important to you. I've given you *every one* of my secrets.

Have you been struggling to find time with your spouse? You'll find practical and tangible ways to spend time together and make your husband feel like a priority again. Need help with organizing your house? My ideas are easy to carry out and will help you find order in the midst of chaos. Once you read this book, you won't be able to wait to get your priorities in order and experience the peace that comes with knowing you're not pulled in every direction anymore. You'll be able to order your life the way you want to instead of letting life order *you*.

This book is an easy-to-read handbook you'll want to reference over and over again. At the end of each chapter, I've included action points that will make prioritizing your life a breeze. By following my fun and easy suggestions, you'll be able to balance your priorities and feel confident you can handle your responsibilities.

Don't be the mom who continues to struggle day after day, trying hard to pull herself out from under the mountain of laundry, the one who doesn't enjoy teaching anymore because it's too overwhelming. Be the mom who balances her priorities well. Be the mom who confidently smiles at her priorities and knows she's got this, the kind of mom others see and say, "I don't know how she does it all."

Don't wait to read *The Homeschooling Housewife*. You have kids who need you to get your life in order, and your hungry husband is counting on you to defrost the meat. You need to have your priorities in order now. Don't let another day go by not knowing what to do. The actionable tips you're about to read for juggling your priorities have been proven to create order, peace, calm, and joy. They will take away your feelings of overwhelm. All you have to do to stay in control of your priorities is keep reading. Each chapter will give you new insight as you strive to find the balance of juggling it all, one priority at a time!

Much love in Christ,
Amber

Chapter 1
Balancing the Priority Of Putting God First

"As God is exalted to the right place in our lives, 1,000 problems are solved all at once."
~ A.W. Tozer

When I was 16 years old, I was an exchange student in a small town in Mexico, nestled deeply in the mountains in the Southern part of the country. To get to that town, I had to ride on a charter bus. The roads in Mexico are tight and narrow, and most don't even have guardrails. One glance out the window was enough to make me almost lose my lunch. If you've ever been to Mexico, you know the traffic rules aren't a high priority. It was common for the driver to shut off his lights and glide into the other lane while going around the corner of the mountain. That way, he wouldn't fall off the side of the mountain, and he could see if anyone else was coming in the other lane.

That makes sense, right? Wrong! It terrified me! I had no idea where I was, where I was going, or how much pain would be involved in the process. I had two choices: I could sit in fear the whole time and worry about whether or not the driver knew what he was doing, or I could sit back and enjoy the ride, trusting that the driver of the bus was in control and he would get me safely to my destination. It was an exercise of faith.

Homeschooling starts with faith…a lot of faith. In fact, much like my bus ride, homeschooling has scary turns and times of uncertainty, but also the thrill of the ride. If I were to ask you why you wanted to homeschool, you would probably include your faith somewhere in the answer. Do you want to teach your kids how to have faith in God? Do you want to leave your faith as a legacy for future generations? Is the act of homeschooling simply a step of faith? Does it leave you shaking in your boots? Throughout reading this book, you'll have a chance to answer these questions and more, but I encourage you to begin answering them now.

You're the Best Example of Faith for Your Kids

Homeschooling your children isn't just about teaching them academics. You teach your kids every day simply by your actions, and the fact that you're around your kids for a significant amount of time means they'll be learning primarily from you. Your kids need to see that you have a deep faith in God. They'll look to you and see what your response is when times get tough.

How do you handle difficult circumstances? What's your reaction when you're afraid things aren't going the way you want? Do you trust God with your whole heart? Whatever your response is to adversity, your kids will see the example you set. You'll teach them to either have a deep faith in God or to fear when they don't understand something. Your example of faith may mean they learn to trust God even through the rough times of uncertainty.

I love the phrase, "More is caught than taught." You can talk to your kids about what faith looks like until you're blue in the face, but ultimately, what you do is what they will learn. If your faith needs strengthening, that's okay. Everyone needs to grow. First, consider your time with the Lord.

Your Own Daily Quiet Time is a Must

Having an effective quiet time on a daily basis is, by far, one of the most important things you can do for yourself and your family. When you spend time in God's Word, you'll be able to handle life and all it throws at you. It's like being rejuvenated every day! If you haven't developed the habit of meeting daily with God, I'd like to encourage you to start right away. Don't let another day go by without opening the Word and feeding your soul from it.

If you've been a believer for any length of time, you know the Bible is pretty specific when it talks about spending time in Scripture. God tells us that in order to grow, we must abide in Him. In John 15:4-5, Jesus said that apart from Him, we can do nothing. We *must* be in God's Word, and it *must* be daily, but why is it such a struggle to spend time in the Word? It's the very source of hope and encouragement in our lives, yet it's often the first thing to get set on the back burner, and the last thing to get placed back into our schedules.

Sometimes, it grieves my heart to think I'd forgo spending time with the One who loves me most. My God and my Creator is offering His heart to me, and there are many times I pass it by for lesser things, "but He answered, "It's written, 'Man shall not live by bread alone, but by every word that comes from the mouth of God.'" (Matthew 4:4 ESV). God knew what He was doing when He said we would need His Word. We need it like we need food. In order to thrive as believers, we need a direct connection to God. He's our life source!

Sometimes, I wonder what would happen if I ate food the way I consume the Bible. It doesn't take me long after skipping a meal to run ravenously to the kitchen in search of nourishment. Give me a day, and I can barely function. I can't imagine going a week without satisfying my stomach. It would be incredibly difficult to function without food for any significant length of time. If you imagine, for a moment, that the Bible is food for your soul, and you follow my illustration, you can apply what I am talking about to your heart.

I'm ashamed to admit there are days, if not weeks, I can go neglecting God's Word. What happens to my heart as a result isn't pretty. I become spiritually starved and can't function. When life throws its difficulties at me, it's harder to stand strong and really fight the battle I am called to fight. Why don't I run ravenously to my Bible in the same way I run to the kitchen when missing only one meal? A starved soul can't serve. I'm not a good wife or mother when I neglect God's Word.

You Can't Run On Empty

What happens when a car runs out of gas? That's an easy answer! It won't run, period. It just won't go. If you've ever been on a car trip and run out of gas, you know there's nothing you can do to make the car move other than to give it more gas. For some reason, we like to trick ourselves into thinking we can go further and further with less and less nourishment for our souls, but eventually, we'll end up sitting alongside the road of life, unable to go any farther.

The same is true of your spiritual life. If you aren't filling yourself with God's Word on a daily basis, eventually, you'll have nothing left to give. It will affect your marriage, your parenting, and your ability to homeschool. Patience runs thin, and emotions run high, when you aren't filled daily with the Word of God. Running on empty has many repercussions. When I'm not in the Word on a *daily* basis, I'm not a godly wife, mom, or friend. I struggle to handle everyday life. Little things that would otherwise not be so difficult become things I can hardly handle. It's amazing how magnified things can become when we aren't in the Word daily.

Change is Easy

Now that all the bad news is out of the way, I want to give you the good news. It's super easy to make a change! You don't have to go on feeling starved spiritually. You can easily start getting into God's Word on a daily basis, and you can do it today! It's not hard to pick up Scripture and just read. You'll be amazed at the difference you feel when you spend time in God's Word.

While you're reading, let the Scripture penetrate your heart and see the difference it makes in your attitude and state of being. For me, feasting on God's Word, especially after a famine, is like finding water in a dry and thirsty land. I feel like I can't get enough, and it's hard to understand why I ever waited so long to get back into the Bible. It feels so good to commune with the Creator.

Later, you'll see the method our family uses and how it ties into our family worship and involves everyone.

You Need a Quiet Time to Refresh

As a homeschooling mom, your Quiet Time is going to look a little different from that of a seasoned believer who's retired and doesn't have kids running around. In some ways, you'll need to grab any time you can get. It's hard to find a structured time to sit and study God's Word when you're home with your kids all day long, and I think God understands that. He takes our best efforts, and He blesses them and multiplies them. You might not be able to find the same time every day to spend time with God, but what I want you to focus on is finding *any* time at least once a day. Don't let the sun go down before spending time in the Bible.

I wish I could tell you to find the perfect set up in the perfect location at the perfect time each day, with your warm cup of tea or coffee, to study God's Word, but you and I both know the life of a homeschooling mom will likely never look this way. Don't wait until you find the perfect location or time of day to start digging into the Bible. Start digging in now. One trick I've learned over the years is simply to keep my Bible open on the kitchen counter so I can find a verse to look at as I fly through the kitchen trying to feed people throughout the day. Maybe I'll only have two minutes after clearing the table and putting away the dishes, but I can read a verse and meditate on it while I finish cleaning up from dinner.

I've found that one of the most difficult things to overcome in having an effective Quiet Time is figuring out what to read. This seems to be even more difficult than actually finding time. (If I'm honest with myself, I can usually carve out at least a half an hour per day that I waste doing something unnecessary.) When it comes to finding a passage, it's not as difficult as it may seem. You may feel as though you need to have the perfect book or the perfect tools in order to study your Bible, but I'm here to say you need to get "perfect" out of your head!

Here are a few ideas to get you started and help you figure out where to start reading in the Bible:

- **PSALMS** – The Psalms are full of hope and encouragement; they're a great starting point when you're not sure where to begin. I'd recommend starting at the first chapter and working your way through the entire book.
- **PROVERBS** – Proverbs has 31 chapters, which makes it an excellent book to read in a month. Read one chapter for every

day of the month. Don't worry if you miss a day; just skip the chapter and go on to the next chapter that matches the date.

- **THE GOSPELS** – The Gospels are fascinating to read and will teach you all about Jesus' life and ministry while He was here on Earth. Reading the Gospels is how we get to know the person Who is our Savior!
- **THE EPISTLES** – The Epistles are some of my favorite places to read because I'm a very practical person, and I find them to be highly applicable to everyday life. They discuss Christian conduct and help believers know what action steps to take in real-life situations.

I'd advise against letting your Bible fall open to any particular passage and reading something random. You want to be intentional about having a good Quiet Time and making the most out of it, even if you can't spend an hour a day. Having a daily Quiet Time is important, and it'll show in your parenting whether you have spent time with God or not.

As I mentioned before, if you're running on empty, you won't make the best decisions regarding your emotions or attitudes. However, if you're filled with Scripture, you'll notice a huge difference in your parenting and other relationships. God's Word is a lamp unto our feet and a light unto our path. (Psalm 119:105) When we have Scripture in our hearts, our parenting will be more God-centered and effective.

Bible Memory

Take the time to memorize Scripture. It really is worth it. Since, as a homeschooling mom, you don't have a lot of extra time to meditate on Scripture and sit quietly with your Bible, memorizing passages of the God's Word will be your biggest weapon when you struggle with fears or temptations to have a bad attitude. God said in Psalm 119:11 to hide His Word in our hearts so we won't sin. He knows what we need in order to stay pure in our thoughts and actions.

I'd like to encourage you to write out a few verses that will lift you up as you homeschool your kids throughout the day. Put them on note cards and scatter them around the house. Take a few minutes while you're getting ready in the morning to look them over and begin to memorize them. Put verses in your teaching books and hang them up around your school room. If you see a particular verse every time you go out the door, you'll begin to memorize it without even trying. You can also find a method of memorizing that works for you. Whatever you do, just memorize it!

Now, it's Time to Build Your Kids' Faith

Once you have a good handle on how to grow your own faith, it's time to help your kids grow theirs. You don't have to have the strongest faith or the best Quiet Time routine. But it's important that you lead your kids by example. That's why I suggest disciplining yourself to find a Quiet Time, and then, once you do, you can teach your kids how to have a Quiet Time of their own. Please don't wait years to do this. Start today.

There's no greater inheritance to leave for your children than a legacy of faith. Pass your faith on to your kids, and exponentially, you'll reach more people than you ever could in a lifetime. Teach your kids to love God so they can teach their kids to love God and so on. In doing so, you'll reach people you may never even meet, such as your great-great-great grandkids!

As a homeschooling mom, you'll have many opportunities throughout the day to teach your kids faith. I promise you; there'll be times you'll need to say, "Mom needs to pray right now; I'll be right back." (I've done this while trying not to pull out my hair!) In all seriousness, let your kids see that you depend on Christ for everything. It's okay to let them know you struggle sometimes and that you depend on God to get you through each and every homeschool day.

Look for opportunities to teach your kids about God and His grace toward us. Show mercy, and connect it with His love for us. When you're tempted to be angry with a child who's being difficult or not understanding something, remember God's gift of grace toward you and then show it to your child. Use mistakes to teach. Display your faith. Let your kids see you have a real faith that runs deep and is genuine.

Teach About Missionaries

What better way to teach your kids what true faith is than to teach them about missionaries? True missionary stories are a great way to show faith in action. I've always been fascinated by some of the stories missionaries have to tell. There are countless, amazing stories of real missionary families having no choice but to trust God. Your kids' faith will grow as you tell them stories of what others have done to make sacrifices for God.

Teach your kids to pray for missionaries and make it part of your daily school routine. It's great to instill a habit in your kids of praying for those who are serving in the ministry. You can talk about specific missionaries throughout the day, and when your children pray for them by name, they won't just be faces on a prayer card hanging on the bulletin board at church. They'll be real people. I like to make one day of the week missions-focused. For example, on Wednesdays, our family likes to read *Window on the World* by Daphne Spraggett and Jill Johnstone, which talks about different countries and the efforts missionaries are making to bring the Gospel to unreached people groups.

You can highlight a certain missionary your church supports, or, if you're in need of finding someone to pray for, check out *Voice of the Martyrs* at persecution.com. These are real people who need our prayers, people who have sacrificed everything, including their daily comforts and lives to share the Gospel. It doesn't get more real than these stories.

Talk to your kids and have them imagine what it would be like to sit in an empty jail cell with nothing but the clothes on their backs...no Bible, not much for food, unclean facilities. Have them imagine the sacrifice. You can serve beans and rice for dinner one night and teach your kids about the sacrifice some of the missionaries are making so others can hear the Gospel. Also, remind them that this is a great reason to memorize Scripture. You never know when one day you might not have your Bible with you. Hopefully, it's not for these reasons, but you'll want to be prepared just in case.

A few years ago, a certain missionary was imprisoned for his faith, and we talked about him so much that my then 5-year-old began to pray for him every day. Not a night would go by without him mentioning that we needed to pray for this pastor. Our little boy diligently and faithfully prayed for him at mealtimes, bedtime, and when he woke up. Imagine the tears that were in my eyes when I was able to tell my son that God answered his prayers. The missionary he had lifted up in prayer for so long was now home. Talk about growing his faith – and mine!

Another missionary story that forever changed my life was Gracia Burnham's story called *In the Presence Of My Enemies*. I highly recommend this biography if you really want to grow your faith. I could find little to complain about after reading the story of how she and her husband were captured by guerrillas in the jungle of the Philippines, all for the sake of the Gospel. It completely changed how I viewed the disappointments and inconveniences of my life.

You may have other stories of missionaries that have really challenged your faith, and I highly recommend you share them with your children. It's easy to make it a part of the homeschooling day. That's the privilege we have as homeschooling moms. We can teach curriculum that stimulates our kids to grow in their faith. Missionary stories encourage our faith by seeing how others live out their faith in a very real and tangible way. By teaching our kids about missions, we make faith a priority.

Find a Child to Sponsor

A great way to teach kids to exercise their faith and to develop an awareness of others is to sponsor a child in an underdeveloped country. There are many kids in need of financial, physical, and spiritual support, and there are many agencies available that are spreading the Gospel as well as feeding kids and meeting their basic needs. Just make sure you choose one that's first committed to spreading the Gospel. Also, be sure to check that the majority of their funds are allocated toward the children and not the agency. You can work on jobs together as a family to raise money. Your kids could also earn an allowance that they could use to help support the child. Maybe your kids could even look for a job helping out a neighbor with yard work in order to help cover the cost of sponsorship.

Our family has really had fun working with Samaritan's Purse in the Operation Christmas Child program. We've enjoyed reading Franklin Graham's book, *Operation Christmas Child: A Story of Simple Gifts*, together as a family throughout the year. Usually, my husband or one of our older kids will read a chapter out loud after supper. Then, we talk about the chapter and what it must be like for some of the kids as they receive their shoe boxes.

I keep a half-gallon mason jar in our office for the kids to drop change in throughout the year. It keeps the mission before us, so we're constantly remembering to pray for Operation Christmas Child and to sacrifice a little bit by giving our change. If I find money in the dryer, it goes in the jar, and the same child who prayed diligently for the imprisoned missionary also runs his own "OCC Campaign." He meets his grandparents at the door with the jar in hand, gives a small statement about the mission and how the kids need our help and then collects whatever change Grandpa has. It's sweet to watch, and it's evident God is building a care and concern for others in his little heart.

At the end of the year, our church participates in an OCC packing party, and we're able to donate the money we've collected to help with the cost of shipping boxes. Also, our older children have enjoyed going to the packing center in Minneapolis to help get the boxes ready to send out. There are many opportunities to serve with Operation Christmas Child, and it's fun for the whole family.

If you simply want your kids to know about other countries and the work being done there, I highly recommend *Window on the World* and *Operation World* by Jason Mandryk. Both of these books are a great way to expose your kids to new cultures. You can commit to praying for the prayer requests listed for each country. I recommend getting a map and talking about where these countries are located. You can also talk about the privileges we have as believers compared to how others suffer.

Make Faith a Priority through Family Worship

Family Worship is the meat and potatoes of your faith. It's the point where you actually get to show your kids *how* to live out their faith in God and a great way to keep a real sense of God in your life throughout the entire week. It's easy to keep God in a box we take out only on Sundays, but if you want to teach your children that faith is real, they'll need to see it between Sundays, every day of the week.

The method we have used in our family ties in to our kids' personal Quiet Time. We've found the best method is to choose a book of the Bible and have our kids spend their personal Quiet Time reading a chapter in that book. My husband and I read the same passage during our Quiet Time. Here is what it looks like fleshed out:

After lunch is cleaned up, and the littles are laid down for a nap, when the house is nice and quiet, the big kids each find a quiet spot somewhere alone. They each read the chapter for the day, and they use the S.O.A.P. method to dig into the Word.

- **Scripture**: Read the passage of Scripture.
- **Observe**: Consider what the passage is saying.
- **Apply**: Consider how this passage applies to me.
- **Pray**: Spend time in prayer.

Then, after dinner that evening, we read the Scripture passage together - the same passage the kids used during their Quiet Time. This is also a great time for our beginning readers to start practicing their reading-aloud skills.

We take turns reading aloud, and then we ask each child to share with us what their favorite part of the passage was. It can be a verse that stood out or something they learned in their Quiet Time. Then, we discuss it and answer any questions that may have come up during their personal reading. This method works well because it keeps continuity within our family. We have the little kids who can't yet read, participate by using a Bible picture book they can quietly look through as we do Family Worship.

During Family Worship, we use the acronym W.O.R.S.H.I.P. to keep us on track:

- **Word**: We read the Word together.
- **Observations**: This is the time the kids tell us their favorite verse or verses and what they learned while reading.
- **Rejoice**: We rejoice over the ways God is using His Word in our hearts to change us.
- **Sing**: We use our TV and YouTube to help us out, since our family isn't overly musical. At the beginning of the week, we divide our kids and assign them the job of picking out praise songs for us to sing together. We ask them to find songs that display the lyrics so we can all sing together. They pick out one new song, one old favorite, and one song the little kids will like. This method works out well and gives the kids a part in our Family Worship time.
- **Highlight**: This is the time we take to highlight something special we want the kids to know or remember. Sometimes, it's a missionary; other times, we might want to discuss a way we have seen God work in our lives. You can choose anything you would like to talk about during this time. It's a really neat time to get your kids talking about God!
- **Instruct**: We use this time loosely to cover something we want to teach. It could be a character trait or a time to discuss a hot topic. We also like to use it as a time to discuss ethics questions (more about that later).

- **Pray**: We spend time asking the kids for praises and prayer requests, as well as answered prayer. In doing so, we help them see the importance of prayer.

Make it Real

While these are practical ways to teach your children about faith, I want you to teach your kids that your faith is *real*. It's okay for them to see you struggle in your faith. It's okay to let them know that sometimes you're confused or that you're having a hard time trusting God. It's great for kids to see you trust in God as you go through struggles.

A wonderful way to show them exactly how this is done is to talk about what God is doing in your life. Share testimonies of how you see God working. One of the greatest blessings I've ever received as a mom happened while I was in a time of difficult struggle. My eleven-year-old son came up to me and asked, "Mom, can I pray for you?" He knew that faith in God is real and that when we're struggling, we go to Him. He knew this because that's what we've *taught* him and *shown* him. He knows that when we aren't sure what path to take, we pray and ask God for direction.

The best way to teach your kids to have faith in God is to let them see it in your life. When your kids see that you have a real faith in God, they're more likely to trust and follow Him themselves. Faith will become natural, like something they have always known. It'll become an extension of their very being.

Consider sharing your testimony of how you came to faith in Christ. Your kids will enjoy hearing how God saved you and you may even use it as a way to introduce your kids to the gospel.

Prayer is the Natural Outpouring of Your Faith

Prayer is the connection between your faith and God, and believe me when I say, "As a homeschooling mom, you'll pray a LOT!" Kids have a way of making you go directly to the Throne of Grace! I find it funny that being a homeschooling mom makes me pray more now, than ever! Sometimes in anguish, sometimes in desperation, and sometimes in fear, for whatever reason, prayer is definitely a vital part of homeschooling. 1 Thessalonians 5:17 (NIV) says, "Pray without ceasing." Teach your kids that God wants us to have a never-ending prayer.

Have you ever had a dry cough or a tickle in your throat? You know, the kind that constantly needs a little cough in order to make your throat feel better? It feels like all you do is cough quietly all day long. This is the same idea as praying without ceasing. When I understood this, it was a great relief to me. You see, as a homeschooling mom, I don't have time to pray for hours a day on my knees in a prayer closet, although I'd love it if I did! I find the cough illustration encouraging.

In the same way a dry throat makes you cough little coughs all day long, you should constantly be having little conversations with God, all throughout the day, almost without even realizing it. Once I heard the illustration about coughing, I started calling them prayer coughs. You can have a prayer cough all day long, and it never ends.

Prayer Keeps You Connected to Your Life Source

Prayer is the direct line of communication between you and God and it's important because it'll keep you connected to Him. Pray about everything. Whether it's the start of the school day or the start of the school year, prayer should be at the beginning.

First, prepare your heart for teaching by asking God to keep your attitude Christ-like. This is a big deal as you homeschool kids who might know how to push your buttons. I've found that if I start my day with prayer, I'm much more likely to keep my attitude in check. It's also a good idea to start the school day with prayer and include your kids. I like to call on a different child each morning to start our homeschool day with a prayer. It gives him or her practice praying publicly and teaches the importance of going to God for everything.

Ask your kids to take a minute to share any prayer requests or things that might be on their mind. Also, take time to talk about any praises and answers to prayer they may have received. Teach your kids to pray about everything. If they're struggling with a test or a particular subject, pray with them. Nothing is too small for God!

Prayer should be laced throughout every homeschool day, but prayer should also be at the heart of choosing your curriculum. Have you ever thought about asking God to direct you to the right curriculum for your family? (In Chapter 11 we'll discuss choosing curriculum in depth.) After all, He knows every one of your needs. God knows your budget better than you do, and He knows your children better than you do, too. Before choosing your curriculum, commit time to asking God to show you what He wants you to teach your kids. If you're struggling to find the right math curriculum for your child, commit it to prayer.

I've found that, as I've trusted God with choosing my curriculum, He has given me peace. Now, it doesn't mean that because I've asked, God has given me a supernatural curriculum that miraculously teaches itself. Rather, He has given me the peace to teach the curriculum He leads me to. There've been some pretty incredible ways God has led me to the curriculum He wants me to teach. My first year of teaching, He provided the curriculum for free through a friend of a friend. Also, just because God provides the curriculum, doesn't mean it's always going to be easy to teach, but God gives grace and strength when you need it.

Pray for Your Kids

One of the greatest privileges and responsibilities we have as parents is to pray for our children. As we stand before God, pleading for our children, He hears us. As a parent, you have a great honor to pray for your kids. Sometimes, it can be hard to know exactly how to do that. Praying for my kids is too broad a concept for me. I need a more concrete plan - an organized way to do it, so I want to teach you an intentional and effective way to pray for your kids. All you need is a basic notebook and pen.

First, you'll want to dedicate a section of your notebook to each of your kids, or, perhaps, you might even want one notebook per child. The first thing you'll do is write your child's name at the top of a page. Then, section off the page into two sections, one on top of the other. Under the child's name, write 'praises', and, in the next section, write 'prayer requests'. My husband and I enjoy doing this together, but you can easily do it separately as well.

Sit quietly and without interruption while you think about *one* particular child. At this point, I want you only to think about the positive qualities and characteristics of your child. Try to keep your mind from wandering and thinking about your relationships with your other children if you have more than one. Make this a time when you won't be interrupted because it's important you make a thorough evaluation of each child.

Next, write down everything you're thankful for regarding your child under the 'praises' section in your notebook or binder. Don't be afraid to write down little things as well – they're important too. If you feel you have seen some positive characteristics in your son or daughter recently, write them down. Not only will you have time to praise God for your child's characteristics, but if you find that you haven't been able to appreciate your child as much as you should, this will help you feel like you can focus more on his positive traits.

Next, I'd like you to think about *all* the areas in your child's life that are of concern. These could be problems with attitude or character, or maybe you simply need direction for how to parent your child. Is your child strong-willed? Have you had trouble with obedience? Is your child older and in need of prayer for direction in making good life choices? Does he or she need salvation? Do you want God to convict him or her to be baptized? Is he struggling with a particular subject in school? Whatever the case, this is the time to write down *all* the things you'll faithfully be committing to pray for. Keep in mind there's really nothing too little to ask God for.

I remember a time when we were struggling with a bad attitude in one of our kids. We wrote it down and faithfully began to pray. It was awesome to see God answer our request. Something that's important to note is that sometimes God changes the child, and sometimes He changes *our* hearts toward our child.

Include Your Kids if They're Old Enough

When your kids are little, they may not understand as much. Although it's still okay to talk to them and let them know you're praying for them. Your older kids will have more of an understanding of what you're doing and there's something special about being able to include him. I don't recommend showing him the list you're making, since he may feel awkward about your specific requests. However, that doesn't mean you can't include him.

Plan a time that's distraction-free and tell your child you're developing a plan to pray specifically for him. At that time, ask if there's anything you can pray for him about. Does your child have any fears? Or struggles at school? Is there anything he would like to praise God for? Ask your child to share any concerns he has that he would like to pray for. There's something special about knowing your parents are praying for you that brings security and encouragement. We want our kids to feel encouraged by the knowledge that we're praying for them daily.

Record Answered Prayer

Write the date down beside each entry and pray faithfully that God would answer your request, but then please remember to record when God *answers* your prayer. It's encouraging as a parent to be able to flip through your prayer book and see the ways God has worked in each of your children's lives.

Be Patient

Maybe you're struggling with feeling like you've prayed for your child for a long time and God hasn't answered. Please be patient and keep praying. Scripture says, "The prayer of a righteous person is powerful and effective" (James 5:16b NIV). God does hear you, and He knows your heart. He doesn't always promise to answer the way we ask, but He does ask us to keep praying continually, and we must remember we don't know God's timing or His plans. It's exciting to watch as God hears and answers our prayers and also as He asks us to practice patience if He doesn't answer in our timing.

Something worth noting is that we fall into the trap of praying as though God were our genie in a bottle. We pray, "Your will be done," but we act like God is at our service. What happens when God doesn't answer your prayers? How do you respond?

God, Change Me

A wise, veteran homeschooling mom once told me a testimony that nailed me between the eyes. I had been struggling with our sixth baby who *never* slept. Not at all. I poured out my heart to her as I told her how discouraged I was that God just *wouldn't* answer my prayer.

I told her I had asked God many times to make my baby sleep. It wasn't a huge request. I wasn't asking for world peace or a million dollars. I just needed and wanted to sleep. After all, sleep is something God even commands us to do, so I couldn't understand why he wouldn't honor my *one* request...or was I treating it like he wasn't granting my one wish? When God didn't answer my prayers for my baby to sleep, I got angry and frustrated to the point of not wanting to pray anymore. My pure, raw, and probably very tired thoughts weren't very God-honoring.

As I poured out my heart to this sweet lady, she told me a story. She and her husband had gone on a mission's trip to Guatemala, and when they got there, they fell in love with a very handicapped, *completely* needy child who couldn't even stand by himself. This couple should have been at the end of their parenting, yet they adopted a nine-year-old little boy who needed the love of Christ more than ever. He was stuck in a wheelchair unless they were able to stand up and hold him, supporting all his weight.

In addition to all his physical needs, he also experienced severe insomnia, due partly to the physical issues he faced and partly to the trauma of all he had experienced in Guatemala. Now, one would think that if a couple was honorable enough to adopt a child who was so needy, God would at *least* let him be a sleeper so they could rest at night, but God had other plans, and maybe His plans with this child were simply to allow this little boy to be an example to change my heart. The boy's mom told me about sleepless night after sleepless night. No matter what she tried, he would cry, scream, and thrash all night long. Her husband worked at night, so she was on her own, trying to make it through the night in complete sleeplessness. She had no one there to help her.

Then, she told me something that forever changed the way I thought about prayer. In fact, I doubt she will ever know the impact her words had on me. She told me that instead of praying that God would make their little boy sleep, she prayed that God would strengthen her and encourage her to get through the sleepless nights with love and grace.

I was flabbergasted. "Why wouldn't you pray that God would make your son sleep?" I asked.

She answered me that God's grace is sufficient, that through the sleepless nights, she knew she *had* to rely on God in order to make it through. There was no way around it. Her strength wasn't enough, and the next thing she told me changed me even more. She told me that God *did* give her the grace to make it through. He never made her son sleep, and He never made the physical trial any easier, but her heart was forever changed, and so was mine. I've told that story many times since, and I am still in awe of the way God uses it in my heart every time.

My friend, I am sure you've been there, pleading with God for help when a child has gone astray. Maybe your prayer is that God would rescue you from your financial situation, or perhaps you're facing a physical illness or a trial that seems insurmountable. Maybe homeschooling seems more than you can handle, and you're ready to give up. Maybe you feel inadequate, like you're not cut out to teach your child, but God is reaching out to you and telling you His grace is sufficient for you as well, just like He was for my friend, just like He is for me.

The Game Plan:

- Pick a book of the Bible and start reading. Start developing the habit of reading daily, and if possible, at the same time each day. If you have to, leave your Bible out and open so you can read little verses of truth throughout the day.
- Pick three verses to meditate on and write them on 3"x5" index cards. Look at them at various times throughout the day and discipline yourself to think about them.
- Commit those verses to memory. A favorite way I learned to memorize is to write down the first letter of each word on an index card to act as a trigger for my mind to remember, without seeing the entire word. Then, I say the words while holding the card in my hand. Eventually, I try to say it without looking at the letters. It helps jog my memory and makes memorizing easier.
- Choose a missionary for your family to pray for. Learn about the geographic location in which he or she serves. Write to that missionary and ask for prayer requests and praises. Remember to talk often about your missionary with your kids.
- Develop your action plan to pray for your kids. Choose a notebook and set aside a time to think about how you want to pray for them.
- Teach your kids to have their own Quiet Time. Purchase a notebook and a Bible for each of your kids and help them use the S.O.A.P. method.

Chapter 2
Balancing the Priority
Of Loving your Husband

"Always strive to give your spouse the very best of
yourself, not what's left over after you have given
your best to everyone else."

~ Dave Willis

Your Husband is your primary relationship. Under God, he's the
most important relationship you have. Your kids won't always be
there. There will come a time you have an empty nest, and you'll look
around, and the only ones left in the house will be you and your
husband. What will that be like? Will the two of you seem like

strangers, or will you reap the benefits of cultivating a deep relationship? Will you work hard now, amidst the responsibilities you have as a homeschooling mom?

If you don't take the time to develop your relationship now, you run the risk of finding yourself without any marital relationship when the kids are gone. I understand the challenge. You have kids, and you're trying to homeschool. That's apart from your responsibilities as mom and keeper of the home. It can be difficult to make your husband a priority when you have so many other things vying for your time, but I can't stress enough how important it is that you develop your relationship with your husband now, while the kids are still at home. With kids in the house, it's easy to never have time alone. It's easy to start getting comfortable with the fact that you just don't have time for each other. The relationship you once had can easily be put on the back burner, but if you're not careful, you might wake up suddenly one day as two strangers coinciding in the same house.

Put Your Husband First

As homeschooling moms, we have a lot on our plates. We're busy making lesson plans, correcting homework, teaching phonics, possibly keeping a toddler or two occupied while we teach, and keeping up with all the things it takes to run a household. We're mothering all day long. We're trying to keep up with it all; we're tired and need a break.

It's easy to put your husband last on the priority list, to put everyone else's needs in front of his. I challenge you to do your best to put him *first*. Make him feel special by not allowing things to come before your relationship with him. Before anything else (mom, homeschooler, friend), you're a wife. You're his wife, he needs to know he matters to you and that you're willing to make time spent with him a priority. Here's the thing: When you're in the middle of raising your kids, and if you add homeschooling to the mix, sometimes, you have to intentionally carve out time to spend alone with your husband. It's okay to say no to other things and allow your relationship with him to be primary.

My husband and I make sure to spend time intentionally talking together a couple days each week. (We talk more than just during these times, but this is an intentional, uninterrupted time.) We engage in a laid back conversation, one where we're not working on problem-solving or bill-paying. This is talking on a more personal level. We discuss each other's days, spend time dreaming about the future, and cover any topic in between. When the kids come in and want our attention, we're sure to tell them kindly that we're spending time together. As long as it's not an emergency, we ask our kids to wait.

Your kids will actually feel more secure and more content knowing your marriage is a high priority. Remember, your husband is your primary relationship and your first priority before the kids. There's no reason not to put him first and do your best to honor him by showing him he's a top priority over anyone else.

It's easy to let the kids' schedules get in the way of your relationship with your husband. If you're not careful, you could easily spend your time running in every direction to make sure your kids are happy and fulfilled while losing sight of your marriage. Before you know it, you could become two strangers dwelling under the same roof. Your marriage is worth taking the care to protect. Preserve your marriage by spending time together and building your relationship so it's rock solid.

Have Open Dialogue

As you work to fulfill your husband's needs, you'll have needs of your own that arise. Maybe you're desperate to talk to him, or you need advice for dealing with a difficult child. Perhaps you need a break. Please know it's okay to lovingly let your husband know what you're thinking. He can't read your mind, and it's not fair to expect him to. Keep good lines of communication open, and you'll find it's not hard to tell your husband what your feelings are. If you're careful to carve out special time with your husband, it shouldn't be hard to have good conversation flowing back and forth often.

Date Your Husband

A great way to make your husband a priority is to date him. Not only is it simple, but it's also fun. Think back to when you first met. Chances are, you spent more fun time together than not. You probably made it a point to go out to dinner together, spending time lingering and talking about everything and nothing all at the same time, but as you got busy with kids and homeschooling, dating probably became less of a priority. If it's been a while since you've been on a date, it may seem a little awkward at first, but don't worry. With a little creativity, you'll be having fun date nights in no time.

I understand that homeschooling is expensive, and finances can create a bit of difficulty in dating, but the idea is to spend fun and creative time together. You don't have to break the bank. Try doing an in-house date night. My husband and I enjoy finding a new recipe we've never cooked and then making it together. We even make the grocery shopping trip together an outing. Grocery shopping can actually be a fun way to connect with each other. When you're finished, you can even grab a coffee together after you shop.

Once you have gathered your groceries, block off a night of the week and start cooking together. If you have little kids, it's best to put them to bed for the night and start your date when they're asleep. If your kids are older, let them know the kitchen is off limits because you're having a date night. By cooking at home, you'll save yourself a ton of money, but it's also fun to flirt together in the kitchen as you prepare food together. You might even find your husband has an inner chef he's been hiding!

Bedtime is Important

In order to build your marriage, you need quality time together to talk without being interrupted. With kids around and the responsibilities housewives have, it can seem almost impossible. You might feel like you never get a moment for the two of you to be alone together. I have a simple solution. Your kids need a bedtime. Without it, you may never find the time to talk.

It's not as difficult to put your kids to bed when they're little, but my kids are starting to get bigger, and an 8:00 bedtime doesn't cut it anymore. To remedy this, we let our kids listen to audio dramas in their bedrooms at night. They have to be tucked into their beds when the episode starts and not get up when it's over. In other words, we don't do bedtime twice. Once they're tucked in, we have time to talk without being interrupted. Of course, kids are kids, and inevitably, they will need something, but your kids need to have a regular bedtime you stick with every night.

Your kids are secondary to your relationship with your husband, so you shouldn't feel guilty for taking this time. Of course, you love them, but they can't be the center of everything you do. Always look to build your marriage relationship first and don't feel guilty about it. Ben and I've always made it a point to go to bed together every night. It's the one time of the day no one needs us, and we can finally relax. Waiting up for each other, though not always easy, has been a huge blessing to our marriage. We spend a few minutes recapping the day and talking about the next day before praying together and drifting off to sleep. It's a small way to connect at the end of the day.

Never go to Bed Angry

Anger can kill a marriage, and it can kill it fast. Scripture is clear that we shouldn't let our anger fester, or it gives a way for Satan to grab hold of a relationship and tear it apart. Anger can sour even the greatest marriage if left unresolved. Like a gangrene threatening to spread and kill, if not dealt with, anger can poison the soul and our marriages. There's a reason God wants us to clear up our matters before we sleep on them (Ephesians 4:26). If an issue isn't handled immediately, it's too easy to wake up to the same crazy cycle the next day, and yes, it's crazy. Anger can make us say, think, and do some pretty irrational things. It seems the longer anger isn't dealt with, the more it can fester, and the more toxic it becomes.

It's hard to *never* go to bed angry, but it's worth it to make sure you're right with your husband before going to bed. There have been many nights my husband and I have stayed up most of the night in order to resolve a difference, and although we're tired the next day, the blessings are well worth it. It's tempting to bury your feelings and not talk about them until later, but if you don't resolve something, it can easily become bigger and far worse than it was originally. Keep current on the issues you have, and you'll see your relationship grow stronger and stronger. At first, it may seem awkward to talk through the things that are bothering you, but it will be better in the end.

When you handle your anger biblically, it doesn't have to fester. It doesn't have to carry into another day. You can put anger to rest and reconcile the relationship with your husband. Our marriages depend on our ability to resolve conflict. Without a proper solution to the issues that come between us as married couples, our marriages will become frail and weakened. We become unable to serve the purpose for which God created us.

Furthermore, since we're commanded as believers not to allow our anger to carry into another day, we must deal with anger as soon as it occurs. Like a rotting piece of meat, anger left unresolved *stinks!* We allow the Holy Spirit to work in our marriages when we're able to reconcile our differences in a loving way and deal with anger in a timely manner. We become more effective and are not hung up by anger. We grow in our faith every time we allow the Holy Spirit to work in our lives and choose not to allow our anger to carry into another day.

Can you imagine what our homes would look like if we took God's Word to heart and made sure to have our anger resolved before sleeping on it? Make your husband a priority by taking care of your conflicts before bed. Keep current on your problems so you don't give them time to grow.

Keep Intimacy Alive

I know that as a homeschooling mom of seven kids, there are days when my head can't hit the pillow soon enough. Sometimes, I feel like I drag myself to bed, and I can barely stay awake long enough to get there. Finding time for intimacy with my husband can fall into the lowest of my priorities. I understand that it's not always easy to make time for each other, but when your sexual relationship takes a back seat, you're giving Satan an opportunity to enter in and steal your marriage.

I once heard someone say, "Don't let Satan slither in bed between the two of you." Stay intimate. We shouldn't deny our husbands our bodies because we're tired or unwilling, and we should be careful not to criticize our husbands. Their needs and our needs are totally different. That's not wrong; this is part of our physical makeup, and this isn't to say you shouldn't clearly communicate your needs and desires to your husband.

How you respond to your husband sexually can have a major impact on his masculinity. Think about it; if you baked a prize cake and proudly offered it to him only to have him refuse it, how would you feel? Let's carry it a step further; what if he ate the cake but complained the whole time he was eating it? In your response to your husband, be sure to build him up and let him know he's your priority.

As a wife, you have a major influence on protecting your marriage. I like to think about it this way: Anyone can cook for your husband. Anyone can wash his laundry. When it comes to things your husband needs help with, there's no limit to who could assist, but *you're* the only one who can tend to his physical needs. No one else. And, really, would you have it any other way?

Busyness can make sex get shoved to the back burner one-hundred percent of the time if we let it! It may sound crazy, but have you ever thought about scheduling intimacy? I don't know about you, but I find that if I don't take the time to schedule things that are important to me, they just don't get done. Scheduling intimate time with your husband may sound cold and sterile, but what happens if a month goes by, and you're never together? Isn't it better to schedule time together that you both can count on? Talk about it and agree you'll do your best to make sure you have intimate time alone with your husband on a regular basis. You could even choose a specific day each week, just make it fun! What if you left him flirtatious sticky notes counting down the days (or hours) until your rendezvous? That will help make it fun and feel like less of an "appointment." Use your imagination and get creative.

I understand that you may be at a point where the whole idea of intimacy seems overwhelming with all the priorities you're already juggling, but please understand that making your husband a priority in your life will be beneficial to both him and you…and your children, for that matter. This could possibly have a greater impact on your marriage than anything else you could do.

Read the Bible and Pray Together

There is something special about reading God's Word together. God has given us His love letter to get to know Him, and as you and your husband grow closer to God, you'll also grow closer to each other. It's amazing how spending time in the Bible together will strengthen your marriage. You'll start to see your ideas and values align. The foundation for your marriage will be stronger as God's Word strengthens you both.

In the same way reading your Bible together is important for strengthening your marriage, so is prayer. Prayer is one of the most intimate things you can do with a person. If you want to see your marriage strengthened, start praying together. I realize this may not be the norm for some couples and might feel awkward at first. Sit down and talk to your husband and ask him if it would be okay if you begin to start praying together. Ben and I make it a point to pray together just before we go to bed. Now, this isn't the only time we pray, but there have been seasons of our life, whether through trial, struggle, moving, babies, tiredness, etc. that as a minimum we have at least had our nighttime praying together to fall back on.

Spend time talking about specific prayer requests and praises and then take the time just before you go to bed to pray with each other. It keeps a connection between the two of you, and it will strengthen both of your faith. As you bow before God together as one, you'll see your marriage strengthened. Together, you can cling to Christ as you ask Him to honor your requests. Make it a point for the two of you to pray whenever God gives you a special blessing, no matter how big or small.

We have bowed our heads in the middle of crowded malls, hospitals, hotels, restaurants, etc. When God blesses us or we need to pray, we just stop and pray.

There are many times and reasons you can pray, and you'll begin to see what's appropriate for the two of you. You'll definitely want to pray about decisions such as how to homeschool your kids, your homeschool budget, your homeschool schedule, as well as various difficulties that come up as you're teaching. Pray when you don't know what to do. Scripture says that if any of you lacks wisdom to ask, and He will give it (James 1:5).

It's also important to pray for your husband. He has a huge responsibility to lead your family, and he needs your prayers. Ask him how you can pray for him and let him know you're his biggest prayer warrior. When you pray for someone, you can't help but build a bond with that person. Make it a priority to love your husband enough to pray for him.

A 1950s Wife??

There is a somewhat humorous article circulating around the internet about a 1950s wife and her responsibilities. She was meticulously tidy and seemed to somehow have everything in order. Her meals were hot and ready the minute her husband walked in the door, yet she somehow had time to fan him in his easy chair while he read the newspaper. I never could figure out how she could accomplish both of these things at the same time! She made sure the kids were quietly playing, and the house was neat and clean. She was iconic as a "good" housewife and mother. She never complained, was always happy, healthy, gorgeous, skinny, well-dressed, and had everything under control.

We laugh at the prospect of being anything close to a 1950s wife, yet there is much to be learned from this Wonder Woman. She adored her husband and purposed to make him a priority. She made it about her husband. From the minute he walked in the door, she honored and respected him. Although it's not likely you or I will ever achieve her status, there is a lot to be learned from this lady of yesteryear.

Be prepared for him to come home. Your husband likely works hard all day and wishes he could be home with you in the comfort of his own home. His job may be monotonous or strenuous, and home should be his haven. Do you make him a priority by making him feel honored when he comes home? Prepare for his arrival by taking care to intentionally ready the house and kids. I'm not saying it has to be 1950s style perfect, but do something special to make him feel welcomed when he comes home. Put aside the projects you're working on and meet him at the door with a kiss and an attentive ear. Be ready to listen to what he needs to tell you and excited to share your news with him. Make him feel like a priority.

Serve him. You don't necessarily have to take off his shoes and recline him in the easy chair while fanning him and serving him lemonade, but find a way you can serve him. Get your creative juices running and think about what needs he may have and ways you can meet them. This doesn't mean your needs should never be met, just that you're intentionally showing love to your husband by serving him. Honor him by meeting his needs.

Pay attention to him and his likes and dislikes. You'll find you can learn a lot about your husband by listening intentionally to him. He might not directly tell you what his wishes are, but if you pay attention, you'll find ways to bless him. Did he mention a favorite recipe he had while growing up? Surprise him by finding a way to make it. Maybe he has a favorite hobby he likes but never gets to spend the time engaging in it. Arrange a surprise outing for him to be able to do it.

Be present in the conversation. Give him your attention and listen to him. Make him feel special. He will know you care because you're concerned about him alone, for a moment.

Look for ways to bless him. Because he's your husband and because you're busy, it might be hard to remember to do special things for him. Pay careful attention and find ways to bless him. Make his lunch for him in the mornings or draw a hot bath for him when he comes home from work. Find things that are out of the ordinary for you to do. You'll be a blessing to him, and he will reciprocate your little blessings with blessings of his own for you.

To Those Who Struggle in Your Marriage - Remind Yourself Why You Married Him

For that matter, sometimes, conflicts in marriage get to a point where you can't even remember why you married each other. Maybe you've tried to resolve your conflict to no avail. Perhaps you find yourself not even liking your husband, so when I say you should make him a priority, you're not even sure if you want to. It may be that you're in a rough point in your marriage. You might feel anger and resentment that seems insurmountable. If your marriage is in a really rocky place, please consider finding biblical help through a pastor or biblical counselor.

Sometimes, you need to step back and start fresh. Remember what attracted you to your husband to begin with. More than likely, there was a point you were in love with this man. It might take some intention and lots of prayer, but with practice, you can begin to love your husband again. First, ask God to give you a *supernatural* love for him and secondly, take action! There are some very specific things you can do to help rekindle the love you once had. Begin with specifically remembering the good times. Keep a journal or some post-its somewhere. Write notes to yourself to remember your husband's good qualities, and if you don't think he has any, ask God to reveal them to you. He will be faithful to show you.

Becki's Story

My friend Becki has a powerful testimony of what it looks like to be married to a man who's wasn't saved. Becki and her husband were both unbelievers when they were first married. In fact, she was a professing atheist and wanted nothing at all to do with a faith in Christ, but God had other plans. Through an interesting series of circumstances, she was saved when her son was just a year old.

Since she and her husband did everything together, she had expected that he would hop on the band wagon and get saved, too! Unfortunately, as she grew spiritually, her husband was turned off from Christianity, and a great spiritual divide begin to occur. This was difficult, since they shared everything together, except for Becki's new-found faith.

Becki dug into God's Word and saw the importance of praying for her husband. She repeatedly brought him Scripture, but she didn't do it to show her husband where *he* was wrong. She wanted to show him the ways *she* had been wrong. As she continued to grow spiritually, she asked him for forgiveness. She made it a point to let him know the times she failed according to the Bible's standards. She never pressured her husband into having a saving faith, but instead prayed for him and lived out her beliefs to the best of her ability. She prayed for her husband over a ten and a half year span, asking God to please save him. She was busy raising four boys without any spiritual leadership. Faithfully, she took them to church every Sunday and tried hard to teach them Scripture. Her philosophy was to do the hard thing, to do what God wanted. Although she was actively involved in her church, her husband rarely joined her.

Becki comforted herself with the fact that when Timothy was mentioned in the New Testament, there was no mention of his father. Scripture says his mother and grandmother had an influence over him, and she hoped that through her faith, God would somehow preserve her boys. She continued to live a life worthy of the gospel, letting her husband see that her salvation was real. She lived out 1 Peter 3, which talks about wives submitting to their husbands, and worked hard to be submissive to him even though he wasn't the spiritual leader of the household. Becki reminded herself that she was responsible to do what was right and that God would bless her for her obedience.

Becki prayed, was faithful, and waited for God to work. Eventually, the issue of homeschooling came up. Becki felt she really wanted to teach her son at home, but her husband was opposed to homeschooling. In fact, he said it would *never* happen and told her not to bring it up again. Becki explained to me that he was adamant about the issue, which was out of character for him. Still, she submitted to his wishes and kept praying. She continued to immerse herself in the Word and stayed faithful at church, all the while continuing to pray for her husband. One Sunday, out of the blue, and through a series of circumstances, her husband was eventually saved. Becki was ecstatic as she saw God answer her decade-long prayer right before her eyes.

Then, she had a different problem. Becki had to figure out the new connection between the two of them and had to learn how to step back and let him lead spiritually. She didn't want to make him feel intimidated by the spiritual leadership she had developed in his leadership absence. In fact, to this day, she still makes it a point to be aware of letting him lead the family.

Eventually, through time, patience, and prayer, Becki did end up homeschooling her boys. I asked her what her biggest piece of advice would be for someone in her shoes, someone whose husband wasn't saved or wasn't on board with homeschooling. Without any hesitation, she told me that the wife's responsibility is to love her husband and to give him the respect he deserves. Regardless of the husband's spiritual position, the wife still has the biblical responsibility to honor him.

Becki said she would encourage someone in her situation to continue to pray for her husband no matter what the outcome and to trust that God is in control. Becki told me she lets her husband know how much she values his opinion and always has, even before he was saved.

The neat part about Becki's story is that at one point in her marriage, after she had been saved, and her husband wasn't, he told her that she wasn't the woman he had married, and that hurt Becki. However, after several years and each of their radical spiritual transformations, he has actually said the same thing. Becki isn't the woman he married, but this time, instead of being hurtful, it's an awesome compliment of her spiritual growth.

I wanted to share Becki's story with you in order to encourage you in case you're in her same position. If your husband isn't in agreement with you homeschooling or maybe isn't a believer, I don't want you to give up hope. The same things I mentioned in this chapter will still apply to you. You may have to tweak them a little bit, but by showing your husband love, respect, and honor, you can be sure God will bless you.

The Game Plan:

- Look for ways to make your husband feel like he's important. Make sure to preserve and protect your relationship by spending time talking. Let him know you care by listening to him and sharing your heart.
- Plan a date night together, whether in-house or out on the town. Make it special by preparing ahead of time. If you decide to do something at home, take the time to choose a meal you can cook together and choose a night to do it.
- Talk about a way to make intimacy a priority. Let your husband know you're willing to guarantee that you can be together at certain times. Decide together which times are appropriate.
- Commit to praying for and with your husband on a regular basis. Let him know you're praying for him and ask him if there is anything specific he would like you to pray for. If your husband isn't receptive to praying together, let him know you're praying for him.
- If your husband isn't saved or isn't in agreement with you homeschooling, respect him and still try to include him. Let him know you value his opinions and go to him often with questions and comments so he knows you trust him.

Chapter 3
Balancing the Priority Of Nurturing Your Precious Kids

"You may speak but a word to a child, and in that child
there may be slumbering a noble heart which shall
stir the Christian Church in years to come."
~ Charles Spurgeon

Kids are a gift from God and one of the greatest blessings we could ever receive as parents, according to Psalm 127:3. When I was growing up, and people asked me what I wanted to be, I always said a wife and a mom. I told people I wanted to have ten kids and actually, I still do. At the moment, I have seven children, and, although I'm quite content, I'd still love to have more.

My Personal Testimony

Let me back up almost twenty years ago and tell you my story. I prayed for my husband since I was twelve years old, and when God sent him to me, I immediately knew he was the *one*. I was excited to start married life with him, and that included motherhood as well. On our honeymoon, I excitedly and naively turned to my husband and asked, "Can we have a baby?"

"Sure!" he replied, "Why not?"

We were so young and naive that, now, just saying that makes me laugh. As if he could just hand me a baby! Six months later, I finally found out I was pregnant. It was a long time coming, in my mind. Now I was finally going to be a mommy! How exciting! I couldn't have been happier. Unfortunately, shortly after I found out I was pregnant, my first pregnancy ended in a miscarriage. I was shocked. We were both heartbroken, but I knew God had a plan. The short version of the long story is that it took me *two full years* before I finally had my first bouncing baby boy.

There were a lot of emotional hills and valleys throughout that time, and my marriage grew strong, while my faith in God grew even stronger. The lessons I learned during that time could be contained in another book themselves. In the meantime, while waiting for my first baby, I made it my hobby to study parenting. You see, whenever God chose to give me a baby, I wanted to be the best mommy I could be. I consumed book after book about parenting and child-raising and did my best to learn everything I could.

The most important thing I learned during my time of waiting is that raising kids is an *absolute* privilege and a blessing, and not everyone will experience the joy of motherhood. That perspective gave me an entirely new outlook on having kids. It helped me to see them as the main event in my life rather than an interruption, so when I finally had kids, I embraced motherhood with arms wide open.

Motherhood is a High Calling

Jesus also saw kids as very important. In Mark 9:37 (NIV), "He said, 'Whoever welcomes one of these little children in my name, welcomes me,'" and if Jesus sees kids as important, so should we. Unfortunately, the world sees kids differently. Kids are not generally seen as a blessing. Sure, there are plenty of people who are madly in love with their kids, but for the most part, our society treats like an inconvenience. Motherhood is under attack.

I've been asked many times what exactly I do all day (eat bon bons and give myself pedicures, of course!) and if I've ever felt like I didn't accomplish *enough* in life. I've felt the stares that come from curious onlookers in the mall when my husband and I walk in with all seven of our kids, and there are always plenty of somewhat humorous comments people make as we walk through a restaurant. Usually, it's something about how crazy we are and if we know how 'that' happens!

The world has diminished motherhood to a lesser calling, but, my friend, I'm here to tell you that motherhood is one of the highest callings you can ever have here on this earth. You're raising kids who will one day impact the world, and right here is where the training starts. Wear motherhood as a badge of honor. God sees you as an amazing person, and what you're doing has eternal value.

No doubt, if you have more than a handful of kids, you'll also find that people have opinions they just can't wait to share with you about your family size or your occupation as a mother. My husband and I've learned to take those comments in stride and handle them with grace. When people feel like they must speak into our lives and say silly comments like, "Wow! You have your hands full," we have started smiling sweetly and saying, "We have big hands, and they're full of blessings!"

I can't stress enough how important it is for your kids to hear you say to others how much they're loved and wanted. Please don't ever respond to the negative comments with agreement, but please also respond with love and grace to those people who feel like they *have* to say something.

There's Only So Much Time

Your kids won't be with you forever. There will be days you wonder how you can make it through the day. You might find yourself dragging yourself to sleep way past your bedtime, wondering how you could ever make it through another day. I understand those days, but I want to encourage you that there *will* be a day you have time for yourself, when you can use the bathroom without seeing little fingers wiggling under the door, when you can eat without interruption, and your food won't get cold, when you can read a book in silence.

We only have so much time to influence our kids before they're gone, and then that's it. Make every day count! Ask yourself, "What am I doing to teach my child about God and His kingdom today? Did I do anything to impact my kids' hearts for God?" I know there will be days I don't do as well, but for the most part, I'm aiming for that goal, and you should, too. We have adopted a phrase in our house. It says, "Life is an accumulation of the little choices you make each day." You might feel like what you're doing isn't amounting to much at all, but if you're pointing your kids toward Christ every day, you're going to eventually grow kids who know who Christ is and who will be ready to act on that knowledge.

Ask yourself if you have had a time today to teach your children about God and His love. If you haven't, that's okay. I just want to encourage you to look for an opportunity to do that before the day is done. It doesn't have to be formal. You can have little conversations with your kids throughout the day. Remind them of the blessings God has given you and talk about answered prayers. Pray with them and ask what concerns they have. Point your child to Christ each and every day. Take your job as a mom seriously and make teaching your kids about God a priority.

A Multi-generational Faith

Did you know the only thing you can take with you to heaven is other people? Think with me for a moment about the descendants you'll have two hundred years from now. The only way you'll ever have an influence over them will be through your children. It's a crazy thing to think I might be able to influence my great-great-great grandchildren by doing a good job of teaching my own children right now, but the goal of a Christian mom is to pass her faith on from one generation to the next, and that starts right now!

As a child, I had a dream to be a missionary. Visions of far-off countries in tropical climates often floated through my mind. I loved to soak up missionary stories, and better yet, when a missionary came home to speak at our church, I couldn't get enough. That was what I wanted to be when I grew up, aside from a wife and mom, of course!

I couldn't wait to reach *millions of people* with the gospel. I memorized every verse that had anything to do with teaching others about Christ's love, and I even thought I'd teach myself another language at the age of eight! Missions were high on my priority list. God obviously had other plans, and I never made it to Zimbabwe. I'm totally okay with that now, but did I lose my vision for missions? Absolutely not! My view of missions has simply changed. You see, as a mom, I have the opportunity to influence generations to come, which is exponentially more people than I could ever reach in a lifetime.

Think with me for a minute about how many people you could reach in your lifetime if you raised three kids who grew up to be believers. If your three kids each raised three kids who loved God and served Him, that would be nine more believers, and if each of their kids had only three kids, and those kids loved God and served Him, then you have reached twenty-seven people with the gospel. That's not even counting any of the spouses your godly kids would have married in order to have their godly kids.

Imagine with me for a second that one of those kids becomes a pastor or even just shared the gospel with someone else. Your faith will have had a direct impact on the Kingdom, simply by raising your three kids to love God and serve Him. If you were able to look out two hundred years into the future, is it likely that your family would carry on the faith you're instilling in your kids

Of course, there are no guarantees, and you can never say yes with absolute certainty, but I know that if you're raising kids who love God and want to serve Him, the chances of your family carrying on your faith are much higher. Your kids will have a much higher likelihood of putting their faith in God, simply by watching how you live it out on a daily basis now! That's a lot to think about! Don't get caught up in thinking you have to do everything right in order to raise godly kids; just teach your kids to love Jesus and to serve Him, and, more importantly, have an authentic faith yourself. ? You can have a huge impact right now. You are serving God by teaching your kids to love Him.

What are my Responsibilities as a Parent?

As a mom, you have several primary responsibilities. The first is to train your children in the discipline and instruction of the Lord. Ephesians 6:4 (NIV) says, "Fathers, do not provoke your children to anger, but bring them up in the discipline and instruction of the Lord," and Titus 2:4 (ESV) says, "And so train the young women to love their husbands and children." These are the two main responsibilities that you have as a parent. Your job is to love your kids and to teach them God's Word, but what exactly does that look like?

Let's start with the training part of your responsibilities. Why is child training so important, anyway? First, God commands it. Second, if you take the time to train your kids, they will be a blessing to you as well as others. Your kids will be a joy to be around and will bring honor to you as a mom. Have you ever been around someone who doesn't train their kids? It can be frustrating.

1. Train them to love God.

If you want to raise kids who love God, you must first love God yourself. You have to demonstrate your faith in your life every day so that your kids see it's real, and, more importantly, that God is real. One of the very best ways you can teach your kids to love God is by discipling them. Maybe you're scratching your head wondering, what exactly does it mean to disciple my children? That's a completely fair question!

Simply put, discipleship means to intentionally pour the Word of God into your children and to teach them to obey it. It's more than just taking your kids to church on Sunday. God has given us children, *and* He has given us pretty specific instructions to train our children in the way they should go. Proverbs 22:6 (NASB) says "Train up a child in the way he should go; even when he's old he won't depart from it."

So what exactly does that mean? It means you're making the Bible an integral part of their daily lives, and you're always talking about God. Deuteronomy 6:6-8 (ESV) gives us a pretty good framework of what discipleship actually is:

> "And these words that I command you today shall be on your heart. You shall teach them diligently to your children, and shall talk of them when you sit in your house, and when you walk by the way, and when you lie down, and when you rise. You shall bind them as a sign on your hand, and they should be as frontlets between your eyes."

You might be wondering what exactly a "frontlet" is. That's a very good question! A frontlet is a decorative ornament or band worn on the forehead. The Israelites were commanded by God to keep the verses He told them were important before them at all times. In other words, to always have them on their minds. The Israelites wanted to be sure to honor God and take Him at His Word; they took it literally and actually wrote the verses on scrolls and then carried them around attached to their heads.

Thankfully, God isn't asking us to tattoo these words across our forehead or carry them around on some kind of a headband, but what He is asking us to do is to constantly have His Word before us every day, and in turn, to teach it to our kids; to bind these Scriptures on their hearts. Basically, He wants us to always think about Scripture first and apply it anywhere we can in our life and in the lives of our kids.

As a parent, you're the one who's primarily responsible for the discipleship of your children. Church is a wonderful supplement to what we as parents can do in the home, but it should never be relied on as the sole source of discipleship. You need to take an active role in bringing up your child in the discipline and instruction of the Lord. Discipleship is also a good way to keep your child in the Word as an adult. Of course, there is no guarantee, but by teaching your kids to make God a part of every day at a young age, you're setting them up to stay on track when they leave your home.

If we don't teach our children to follow Christ, the world will teach them not to. Be an active participant in your kids' lives and don't just sit back and let them learn from the culture around them. Kids are sponges and, good or bad, they learn what's put before them. Now, more than ever, your kids are faced with choices you and I never had to think about as children. You need to make sure your kids are prepared and ready to handle all the decisions they will be faced with making in the future. Discipleship is one of the ways you can be sure you're passing on godly values to your kids in an intentional way. Don't let the world be your kids' teacher. It's important that your kids *know* what Scripture says and how to apply it to their lives. Discipleship is simply an intentional way to teach them.

Let me add a side note to encourage you: You may feel inadequate, like you *don't know it all*. Let me reassure you that *nobody does*. We're all learning. It's completely okay to learn right alongside your kids and even let them know that you don't know the answers. I understand that life gets busy, and adding in one more thing can seem overwhelming, but let me encourage you that discipling your children will have lasting and valuable, not to mention eternal, results. Please don't let busyness get in the way. Do your best to make it a priority to intentionally disciple your kids on a regular basis. On the same token, don't feel like you can't disciple your kids until you have the perfect setup or the perfect materials or the perfect time. As you go about your daily business, you can constantly teach your kids Scripture.

We need to diligently teach our children about God and His Word all day, every day. That means you need to constantly look for opportunities to teach your child. Casual conversation is one of the best ways to continually have God before you.

For example, a simple lesson could go something like this: As you look out your front window with your child, you might see a bird in the tree. Watch the bird for a while and explain to your child that there is actually a verse in the Bible about birds. Matthew says, "Look at the birds of the air: they neither sow nor reap nor gather into barns, and yet your heavenly Father feeds them. Are you not of more value than they?" (Matthew 6:26 ESV).

Then, explain to him that he doesn't have to worry about anything because God said He provides for all our needs, just like He provides for the birds. You can tell him that whenever he sees a bird, he can be reminded that God takes care of all his needs, and he doesn't have to worry. As you can see, discipleship can be informal and used during teachable moments.

When Should You Disciple Your Kids?

As I said earlier, discipleship is something that takes place every day throughout the day, but it's also appropriate to find a more formal time to teach your kids as well. In our home, we use Family Worship as a means to disciple our kids.

You can disciple your kids as it works best for your family, but ideally, it should be at least once a week. If you choose a more relaxed and informal format, it may not be at the same time every week.

You decide what works best for you. It could be added as a part of your homeschool routine, or maybe you would like to take time apart from school to do it. In our house, we have done both formats. Currently, we're using the W.O.R.S.H.I.P. method I mentioned in Chapter One. It has been a blessing to our family.

When you disciple your kids isn't as important as the fact that you *actually do it*. If you're stuck wondering how to start discipling your kids, it's not hard.

You can study a book of the Bible together with your child. Don't worry if you have deficiencies; you can learn together. Go through the Scripture and talk about it. See if there are any words or phrases your child doesn't understand and research them together. Then, teach him how he can apply it to his life.

If you don't want to go through a whole book of the Bible, you could take one verse each time you meet and talk about it together or read a book together. Sometimes, we choose this method. We have our kids read a book; then, we discuss it together. There are many options available. Just choose something you're likely to stick with.

Also, please be sure to pray with your kids. It's important to teach them to go to God with everything. Make prayer the center of your discipleship. You see, you have a mission field right before your very eyes. You can always be discipling your kids. Remember to seize the opportunities God puts before you. Sometimes, those opportunities are fun, such as when your kids are asking neat questions that naturally lead into talking about God and the Bible, and, sometimes, those opportunities come in the form of a disobedient child who needs to be reminded that his sin is offensive to God. Whatever the case, always bring your kids back to the gospel.

And this right here, my friend, is the reason I'm very content not to be an overseas missionary. I have kids to disciple right before my very eyes.

2. Train them to be obedient.

Every parent wants their kids to be obedient. Let's face it, if my kids always obeyed and never gave me problems, my life would be a breeze. Unfortunately, kids are typically not obedient. We need to teach them to be obedient because God's Word commands it.

Years ago, at a Biblical training conference, my husband and I were introduced to the concept of "gumnazo training".[i] I'm so thankful we were because it has forever changed the way we parent. I'd like to teach you the same concept, so you can experience the joy and blessing of teaching your kids obedience.

"GUMNAZO" (goom-nad-zoe) comes from the Greek word for gymnasium, and the basic concept is to train. It has made *all* the difference in how Ben and I parent. It's the secret ingredient to raising kids who know how to listen and obey *and* to do it happily. It works with any age and will make your life so. much. easier! Once I explain the process, you'll see how fun and easy gumnazo parenting is. You'll definitely need to set aside some time to practice it, but it will be worth it! Basically, what you'll do is teach, train, and practice. It's very simple, yet oh, so effective!

Imagine you have just started a new job working in a factory. It's your first day, and as you walk through the door, you find yourself at the head of an assembly line, and things start flying at you. You scramble to figure out how to put together whatever the *thingamabob* is that keeps coming at you, but you're totally unsure how. Why? Because no one ever taught you *how* to do it.

Now think for a minute about your kids. Is this what they might be feeling? Is there constant conflict and frustration in your house? Let me ask you to do an honest assessment. Have you properly taught and trained your child *how* to do whatever it's you're wanting? Whatever the source of conflict (leaving messes, shirking responsibilities, negative attitudes), have you spent time teaching and training your child to act and respond correctly?

If you're frustrated, there's a good chance your kids are too, because, let me tell you, if it was me standing at the head of the assembly line, and I didn't know what to do as things were flying at me, I'd want to walk away and never even try. Take time to train your children. In gumnazo training, you should teach your child *how* to do one particular thing. This is the part when you give him all the instructions and expectations you have for him. Then, you'll train him to do it. The training process involves doing run-throughs of whatever you're trying to teach. Following the teaching and training, you'll practice, practice, practice! You'll take several times to run through whatever it is you're trying to teach. Let's look at an example.

For the sake of illustration, let's say you're struggling to get your kids to go to bed in a way that doesn't feel like you're herding a bunch of goats into a corral. I'll use the example of bedtime throughout my explanation of the process, so you can see how easy (and fun) it is. First, you need to teach your child the process you expect when you say it's time to go to bed. Remember, this is just an example and can be used with any age child, in any scenario. Just pick one area that needs a little work.

I like to walk my kids through and explain each step. For example, I begin by saying, "It's time for bed, I'd like you to put away whatever you're doing and respond by getting up and heading to the bedroom. You'll need to get dressed in your pajamas and use the bathroom. Please brush your teeth and get a drink. Then, I'd like you to get into your bed and wait for me to come and tuck you in." Obviously, this will change depending on the age of your kiddos. "Once in bed, I don't want you to get out of bed. Then, I'll pray with you, shut the lights off, and we will see each other in the morning." This is the teaching phase. You might be saying, "Oh right!" but bear with me!

Next comes the Training phase. I'll then walk through all the steps with them. Don't do this at bedtime. Training works best when done in a *non-conflict time* when you have lots of time to spare.

Now comes the fun part. *After* I've taught and trained my kids what I want them to do, it's time to practice. Make sure you choose a non-conflict time to practice. You definitely want to have kids that are well-rested and ready to learn. If you're in the middle of an argument or a conflict just happened, now isn't the time to work on gumnazo training. Choose a time during the day when you can dedicate a significant amount of time to practice the things you have taught. I'm talking full-on practice. This means you'll say, "Ok, kids, it's bedtime," and then you'll expect them to walk through everything as you have taught them. Yes, this means they will even get into their pajamas!

Usually, our practice sessions turn into lots of laughter. It's kind of funny to practice going to bed at 3:30 in the afternoon! When you take the stress out of a bedtime routine, and there's no pressure to actually get into bed because the clock isn't ticking, you can have a *lot* of fun! This is true with anything you're trying to teach. When it's done in a non-conflict time, you won't have all the emotions that come with a child who didn't listen *again!*

It's important to be patient. Training kids takes time and patience. They don't always get it the first time around. You'll need to have a loving and patient attitude as you teach, train, and practice. Think of something you have had to learn and remember it takes time. I think that, sometimes, the frustration in disobedience comes because we expect our kids to obey something we have never actually taught them. Encourage your child as you go and try really hard to keep your emotions in check. Remember that you're intentionally taking time out during a *non*-conflict time to teach, so hopefully, you'll be able to be more patient.

It's a good idea to figure out some areas that need work and then focus on teaching those areas. What are things you're always correcting? What things seem to come up over and over again? Where do you hear yourself nagging the most? If you pay attention, it won't take long to figure out the things you need to be teaching.

It can be something simple like taking shoes off at the door or hanging up jackets, or it can be something complex, like the bedtime routine or completing homework before doing fun things. Maybe it's an attitude issue. Kids can be taught and trained how to answer respectfully and kindly. You can teach and train whatever areas you see need work in your house. Whenever a new issue comes up that has been a problem, write it down so you don't forget to teach it when you get a chance!

When we do training sessions in our house, we either set a timer for a certain amount of time or we agree on a set number of times to practice. It's also important to keep repeating the process throughout the week. Remember it takes time to build new habits. Full training happens after completing a task over and over again. Practice makes progress! You'll find that, as you work on training your kids to obey, your parenting will become much more enjoyable. Conflict times will happen less often, and you'll enjoy your kids more.

Finally, don't forget to praise progress and reward milestones. You'll be amazed at what a difference it will make in your parenting.

Jake, Stop!

It's so worth it to take the time to teach your kids this process. Sure, it takes time, but in the end, you'll have kids who know how to obey. This training will save you time, and maybe even save their life! When one of my sons was little, we saw the importance of training our kids in obedience first-hand.

We were at the park with our good friends and some of their family when my then-5-year-old saw that his daddy had crossed the road to get a ball out of the trunk. Like any child, he wanted to go where Daddy was. Since he was little, he just bolted and began to run out into the street from between two parked cars. Our friend's brother, who Jake had just met, saw him and yelled, "Jake, stop!" Immediately, Jake stopped.

If we hadn't taken the time to teach Jake obedience, he could have been hit by a speeding car and died. It's always worth the effort to teach your kids to obey. As a homeschooling mom, you already have so much on your plate. Imagine the blessing of having your kids obey because you've taken the time to train them.

3. A loving parent disciplines when their child is wrong.

A parent's responsibility is also to be loving, and sometimes, loving your child means disciplining him when he's wrong. If you've given your child proper training and instruction, it's much easier to discipline him when he knows what he has done is wrong, but let me ask you a question. Do you discipline because *you're* offended or because he has offended God? Unfortunately, it's often tempting to discipline your child because he's annoying you. Evaluate your motives the next time you discipline. Pay attention to the reasoning behind why you discipline your kids.

I want to encourage you to avoid the urge to wait to discipline until he disrupts *you*. Really evaluate and be on the lookout to correct and discipline your child when he has broken *God's* law. It will change your attitude toward discipline and his response when he's disciplined. Take the time to explain to him that he has offended God. For example, when he doesn't obey you, it's sin. The Bible says to honor your mother and father. Therefore, you need to discipline him because he directly disobeyed the Word of God, not so much because he made you upset. Take the time to explain these things, and, eventually, you'll have a child who learns to obey God's Word.

Let me caution you: Whatever form of discipline you use *always* needs to be followed up with love and reassurance. I beg you to please, never ever walk away from a disciplining session while you and/or your child are still angry. If you do, you seal up their heart a little bit each time. Eventually, you'll have lost the openness of your child's heart. If you get nothing else from this chapter, please heed this. You *must* let your child know that no matter how grave the offense, there is always forgiveness and that you and God still love him. It's imperative you let your kids know this. A child can walk around with guilt for the rest of his life if you fail to take this step.

Play More; Praise More; Pray More

Sometimes, as moms, we can become very task-oriented, *especially* as a homeschooling mom. It's easy to only focus on what you want to accomplish with your kids, but sometimes your kids need you to just be a mom. In my early parenting years, I came across a simple phrase that serves as a great reminder to me. "Play more, praise more, pray more." It has been helpful in reminding me not to be so task-driven and focused.

It's okay to step back sometimes and stop being a teacher. Your kids need you to sit down with them and enjoy time just being a mom. Play with them and enjoy them. Ask if they have a game they like and then enjoy playing it with them. Maybe your daughter would love to have a tea party with you, or your son would like you to play Hot Wheels. It's okay to take time out once in a while.

You also need to remember to praise your kids. Again, especially as a teacher, it's easy to be in a constant correction mode, but, sometimes, your kids need you to shut it off and praise them for the things you see they're doing well. If you can't think of anything, try to find at least one thing you *can* praise your kids for.

Of course, they also need you to pray for them, and I think we can all say we could pray more. Be a faithfully praying mom. Your kids need you to be their prayer warriors.

A Wise Woman Builds her House

I understand, as a homeschooling mom, the days can get long, and emotions can run high. There are some days I feel like pulling all my hair out, and I could just scream. For some reason, my kids are the biggest provokers of negative emotions in me. If I'm not careful to have self-control, I can undo my child's heart in a moment. If you're like me, you probably find yourself struggling with anger at different times throughout your school day. Parenting in general, is enough to "get your goat" if you're not careful.

There's a really simple and practical way I've found to help me gain control of my emotions. Proverbs 14:1 (NIV) says, "The wise woman builds her house, but with her own hands, the foolish one tears hers down." We want to be working hard to build our kids up. This simple exercise will help you be aware of your attitude and emotions. In order to do it, you'll need to get a handful of building blocks. Every time you do something to build up one of your children, put a block on top of another. Basically, you'll want to have a tangible way to see how you're building up your house. I recommend keeping your block tower where you can see it all day long. The kitchen is a great place; it's important to see your building throughout the day.

The kicker to this exercise is, when you lose your cool with one of your kids or do something that's not edifying or building them up, you need to take all the blocks down and start over. This will give you a way to see how you're doing with building up your own house. Would your kids say you encourage them and build them up, or do you tear down your house with your own hands? I've found this tower exercise is a sobering experience. There are some days I do really well. Other days, not so much.

Your kids will see your example and eventually begin to mimic it, either way. If you're building up, they're more likely to build each other up, and if you're tearing down, they're more likely to tear each other down. Work to make your own attitude that of being a godly example, so they can do the same.

I have also used this exercise with my kids as a way for them to monitor their behavior. It has actually done wonders for helping our kids encourage each other and get along. It's nice that they can see their progress in a real and tangible way.

Your Kids Need Your Time

In order to make your kids one of your top priorities, you need to spend time with them. You have probably heard it said that kids prefer quality over quantity, but I'm here to tell you that's not true. They need both. I realize that, as a homeschooling mom, you're already juggling so many things, but it's important for you to develop relationships with each of your kids, and relationships come by spending time.

Make a schedule to include one-on-one time with each of your kids. It doesn't have to be a long time, just a special time between you and him. This will build a strong relationship between the two of you, and your child will feel like a priority. In my book, that's a win! It'll be helpful to have this relationship established so that when the time comes, and you need to talk to your kids about sensitive matters, it won't be forced. You'll have built the relationship.

Spending time with your kids is a great way to get their heart. If you have their heart, the rest of your parenting won't be as difficult. Find out your kids' individual interests and then spend time doing them with each child. You may not be a great basketball player, but if you go outside and attempt to shoot some hoops with your son, it will mean the world to him. Maybe your daughter is into art, so you could ask her if you could work on a project together. It might take some investigating on your part to find out what your kids' interests are, and you may even be surprised by what you find out. If you can't find anything to do with your child, agree to learn something new together. Try to find something special you can do with each one of your kids.

Rules without relationship equals rebellion. You have to put the time into your child in order to get your child's heart. Relationship is sort of like the glue that holds everything together. Your child doesn't care how much you know until he knows how much you care. Period. If you try to do any of these other things without a relationship with him, you'll fail. Spending time with your child shows him you're interested in him for who he is. There isn't anything more beautiful than having your child's heart, and there's no better time to start working toward that than *now*! It starts by spending time with your kids.

Don't Become Child-Centered

While it's important to spend time with your kids, it's also important not to become child-centered. It's okay to have things you do without your kids, and you don't have to feel bad about it. This goes back to the importance of having a strong marriage, like we talked about in Chapter Two. You don't want the time you spend with your kids to overtake the time you should be spending with your spouse. As always, seek to find the balance. Remember kids need to sometimes be bored. They don't always need to be entertained, and not every minute of every day needs to be fun-filled. Sometimes, kids need to learn how to get along on their own without being entertained.

What Happens if I don't Like my Kids?

This sounds like a funny question, but I've heard more moms ask it than you would imagine. Of course, you love your kids, but being together all day long can make it difficult to like them sometimes. Little things start to get on your nerves, and suddenly you find you're frustrated with your child. Sometimes, it's for no good reason, and, sometimes, there is a very good reason!

I've found it's especially difficult to overcome frustration when I'm tired, so try starting with the right amount of rest. Then, pray about the relationship. It's important to not only pray *for* your children, i.e. their needs, protection, purity, etc.; I've found it equally important to pray that God would give me the heart to love my kids like *He* loves them. When you pray for your kids this way, something special begins to happen. You actually begin to *love* them like God does! It's amazing! When you see someone through eyes of love, you begin to tolerate more of their quirks and idiosyncrasies, and this is true of any relationship.

Sometimes, You Just Need Support

If we're honest, motherhood is difficult, and raising kids can be frustrating. It's okay to reach out for support. Actually, it's okay to reach out for support even if you *don't* feel frustrated. Sometimes, it's just nice to have another mom to talk to.

A great place to find someone who understands is at your local church. Ladies there are usually willing to lend a shoulder to cry on or a listening ear. Find an older woman who has already raised her kids and ask her to be your mentor. You might also find someone in your family who's a great support, or, perhaps, it will be a good friend. If you don't have anyone physically you can rely on, there are many books that have been written to help you through your child-raising years.

The internet is also a great place of support. You can read posts on my blog at allnaturaljoy.com and the homeschoolinghousewife.org. I have resources dedicated to helping moms find joy in everyday living, and this is but one of many websites created for homeschooling moms.

Do Your Best and Let God Bless

Maybe you feel like you're trying as hard as you can, but things still aren't going right. Do your best to honor God as you raise your kids, and He will fill in the gaps. Have grace for yourself on the days that don't go as planned or you feel like you failed. We all fail sometimes. Don't be hard on yourself for the missed opportunities or mistakes you make. Some days are just hard.

When you have a bad day, you need to know it's what you do next that matters the most. Don't beat yourself up over the failures; pick yourself up and start over. Remember that God is a God of grace, and He doesn't expect our perfection. He just wants our willing hearts. As parents, we will always fail, but if we trust God with the lives of our kids, He will bless our efforts.

Listen to Your Kids

Don't just talk to your kids; listen to what they have to say. Kids want to be heard. They want to know they have a voice and that their voices matter. Listen to your child's heart. You may be surprised by what's inside. Proverbs 20:5 (ESV) says, "The purpose in a man's heart is like deep water, but a man of understanding will draw it out." Ask questions to understand your child. Draw out what he or she is thinking and don't assume you know what it is. I've made that mistake more times than I care to admit. Sometimes I ask myself, "Why didn't I listen before I jumped to conclusions?" When you take the time to listen to your kids, they begin to want to listen to you as well. You'll begin to see them give you their hearts and you'll be able to give them yours in return.

Give your Child Clear Boundaries

When you set clear boundaries, everyone is happier. It's much easier for a child to know what to expect if they know what *you* expect! On the contrary, if your boundaries change with the wind, your child will, too. It's not fair to *not* set a limit and expect that he will know what you're wanting. Set the boundaries and then take the time to teach your child what you mean by them. Spend time training them to stay within the parameters of whatever it's you have decided is a good boundary.

Now is the Time

It's never too early to start implementing these things. Likewise, it's never too late to start, either. Don't believe the lie that your child is too far gone to start getting his heart. You'll find there will be joy in the journey of parenting when you have his heart, and you'll develop a lifelong friendship with your child. What could be more awesome than that?

The Game Plan:

- Search your heart and ask yourself if you see your kids as a blessing. Take time to pray about your demeanor toward your kids. Ask God to give you the right attitude regarding them. Do you communicate love to your kids? Find specific ways to show them that you love them.
- Talk to your kids about God and His Word throughout the day. Train them to love Him through discipleship. Plan a time each week that you can spend intentionally discipling them. If you have several kids who are of similar age, you can group them together, although spending one-on-one time is ideal if you're able. Pick a book of the Bible to study together and then read and discuss.
- Make a schedule of one-on-one time with each of your kids throughout the week. Don't pressure yourself into thinking it needs to be hours at a time. Even fifteen minutes of undivided time will go a long way with each of your kids.
- Practice the gumnadzo principle. Evaluate which areas you see your kids needing to work on regarding obedience. Then plan a non-conflict time to practice the principles explained in this chapter.
- Find a friend who could be a support to you. Get to know some of the ladies at your church or your local homeschool group. Then call on one of them for support and prayer when you need to be encouraged. Remember to be a friend, as well.

Chapter 4
Balancing the Priority Of Serving the Body of Christ

"One of the principal rules of religion is, to lose no occasion of serving God. And, since he's invisible to our eyes, we're to serve him in our neighbour; which he receives as if done to himself in person, standing visibly before us."

~ John Wesley

I know as a homeschooling mom, my days are filled to the brim with activity. In fact, if I'm not careful, I burn the candle at both ends, never stopping to take a break. That's why I'm so thankful that God commanded us to have a day of rest. He knew we needed it. Since we're home all week serving our kids, a day of rest, fellowshipping with our church family is of upmost importance.

Church should be a huge priority for a homeschooling family, yet it can be difficult to stay faithful in your attendance. First and foremost, make sure you're part of a biblically-sound church. Be sure that Scripture is being taught and that you're in an environment where people are encouraging obedience to the Bible.

Homeschooling is a large responsibility throughout the week, and it's easy to want to rest on the weekends. Fight the temptation and make going to church a priority in your family. I understand the temptation to sleep in or rest and relax. Homeschooling is tiring, and giving up a morning can be difficult, but it's *well* worth it.

When there is a choice between church and something else, such as a community activity, a birthday, or a school activity, always choose church. It will help your kids see that you really do consider church a number one priority. If you want to teach your kids to love God and honor Him, being a faithful attendee in your local church is a great way to do it. Your kids will follow your example, and, hopefully, one day, they will also be faithful attenders of a church.

God Wants You There

In Hebrews 12:25, God tells us not to stop meeting together. He knew we would need the encouragement and support of our local church family. Let's face it: homeschooling is hard work, and going to church to worship God and focus your mind on something other than teaching is a welcome retreat. You need to be in church so God can fill your soul, and you can be ready to tackle the homeschool week ahead.

However, please be careful not to let your church attendance become legalism. Don't fall into the trap of thinking that church attendance is synonymous with holiness. Because it's not. You can attend church with the wrong attitude and still be *faithfully* attending. I want church to be a *haven of rest*, a place where I refuel my soul and reset myself for the week ahead, a place where I drink from the springs of *Living Water*, and my soul is refreshed, and I want that for you as well.

Don't be Caught Unprepared

Have you ever been caught on Sunday morning completely unprepared? Have you felt like it's too much effort to get to church?

Maybe you're running around chasing little ones and trying to shove food in their faces as you load kids into your van when you realize one of them isn't even wearing shoes and another has Cheerios on his face.

I've Been There!

Do your Sunday mornings need a makeover? I want to help take the chaos out of your Sunday morning and show you a way that will make your day of worship much more enjoyable. Going to church will be more of a blessing than a burden. There's a simple secret that will help make going to church just a little bit easier.

First, I need you to switch your mindset. Instead of thinking church is all about Sunday, I want you to start thinking that Sunday *starts* on Monday. Get in the habit of thinking about church *all week long*. Prepare for church every day throughout the week. Each day, think, "What's *one* thing I can do to get ready for Sunday?" Take a little time to sit down and make a Sunday morning checklist. Include some things you need to bring to church. Did you promise anyone you would bring a book for them to borrow, or maybe you promised to bring some hand-me-downs for another homeschooling mom? Does your church have a potluck on Sunday afternoons?

Think to yourself about all the things you'll need to bring with you as you're walking out the door on Sunday morning. This might sound silly, but sometimes, during the week, I do a mock walk through, pretending I'm walking out the door for service *right now*. Then, I think about what I'd need to grab if I was really going to church at that very moment. It's amazing what things come to my head during that little exercise; then, I write them on my checklist.

Also, look at your checklist throughout the week and see if there is anything you can do to be preparing for church on Sunday. Keep your checklist closely at hand, maybe even on the refrigerator, so you can refer to it each day. Then, as you're on your way out the door on Sunday morning, a quick glance at your checklist will help you feel much more prepared. You won't be racing back in the door to grab the thank you card you were supposed to write. It will already be written and waiting for you.

On Saturday night, go through a checklist of everyone's wardrobe. I've been caught too many times with clothes that need to be ironed, pants missing buttons, and shoes that are nowhere to be found. Lay everything out Saturday evening. Make sure you include the kids in the process. Have them help by taking responsibility for their own things, then, if you have younger kids in your family, pair them up with the older kids. Together they can prepare all necessary things for church in the morning. Gather everyone's Bibles and Sunday School papers and put them safely in an agreed upon location. Have everyone put any extra things in the same special spot so that in the morning, everything is ready to go, and you won't be frazzled or frantically searching for the important things that slipped your mind.

Talk to your kids about what a privilege it is to be able to go to church. There are people in other countries who can't attend church because it's against the law. So as you prepare your hearts for worship teach them that church is worth preparing for throughout the week.

Plan and prepare as much of your Sunday meal as you can on Saturday night as well. If you've ever done any freezer cooking, this would be a great time to pull out one of your freezer meals. Slow cooker meals are wonderful for Sunday dinners. You never know how long you might be visiting after church, and not having the pressure of something cooking in the oven is a nice feeling. You don't have to worry about it drying out or burning; your slow cooker will be dutifully waiting for you, keeping your food hot until you're ready to eat it.

In addition to preparing for Sunday morning throughout the week, talk about church all week long and get your kids excited about it. Look forward to it. Begin to see church as one of the exciting things you do together as a family. You get to worship God together! That's pretty awesome! When you keep church in your thoughts all week, you also keep the act of worship fresh in your mind. That way, church is just a normal thing you do instead of something extra you have to try to force into your schedule. Just like an exciting trip you might prepare for and talk about for days, get your kids excited and ready for church in the same way. It's worth preparing for!

What to Do on Sunday Morning

If you were careful to do your preparation for Sunday morning throughout the week, Sunday mornings should be peaceful and calm. Of course, there will always be unforeseen circumstances, and people definitely add their own personal flair to the morning. Each person in your house has an impact on how your Sunday morning will go. Sometimes, little attitudes creep in, but if you're prepared with all the details for church, you shouldn't be as stressed, and you'll be able to handle the unexpected things that come up.

There are several things you can do to make your Sunday mornings go even more smoothly. First, keep your breakfast as simple as possible. This isn't the time to make an elaborate brunch and go all out with a large gourmet meal. Save that for Saturday mornings. Try serving cold cereal or even oatmeal. Toast with peanut butter and jelly is also a great idea. Whatever you do, keep it simple.

Some people have special toys that can only be played with on Sundays. Their kids look forward to them all week because the kids know it's something they can only do on Sundays. It's a little touch that makes Sunday seem and feel a little bit different and extraordinary. Try to pick activities like reading or doing puzzles while the kids are waiting for everyone to get ready for church to start. This is also a great time for the big kids to read to the little kids.

Since Sunday morning is a good time to prepare your hearts for worship, avoid turning on the TV, and don't let your kids play electronics. This is a day to relax and refresh. You don't want Sunday to be like every other day of the week; it's special. It's the Lord's Day! I like to carefully choose worship music and have it playing in the background as our family gets ready for church. It makes such a difference in preparing our hearts for worship. Try it and see what I mean. The right music can help you set a worshipful tone in your house. Then, when you arrive at church, your hearts will already be softened to the Word of God.

What's Our Attitude Toward Church?

Did you know that there are at least 51 countries where church is illegal, and the government is hostile toward Christians? It's hard to believe as we walk to our cars and safely head to church. We don't really contemplate the privilege it actually is to go to church in a free country. We're blessed to be able to be a part of church. Back in Chapter One, we talked about missionaries who are risking their lives every day in order to share the Gospel. Remind your kids that not everyone gets to go to church without fear. If you change your perspective on church, it can make you feel more appreciative and less like church is just one more thing to add to the schedule.

Maybe you don't struggle with the priority of church. That's awesome! I'm rejoicing with you that you see attending church as a gift.

It's About the Relationships

If you really want to feel like a part of your church, you can't just sit on the sidelines. If you slip in and out of your church quietly on a Sunday morning, you'll never really feel involved. There are some practical ways to feel like your church is more than just a place you visit on Sundays where nobody really knows your name. Make it a priority to get to know your pastor. Think of creative ways you can bless him. Figure out his favorite snack and drop it off one day during the week, but be sure to bring your kids along so they can have a part in it as well.

When I was growing up, my parents encouraged me to talk to my pastor and ask him any questions I had about the Bible or his sermons. I'm so glad they did because it opened up the lines of communication, and I became comfortable talking to him. I didn't feel like he was some unapproachable guy. As a result, I also became much more interested in church. I felt like if I had a connection to the pastor, I had a connection to the church. Become a friend to his wife as well. Invite them over for dinner and make them part of your life. The pastor and his family are real people and will likely enjoy your fellowship.

Next, get to know others in the church. Host dinners at your house. It's a good idea to invite more than one family so they can get to know each other while you get to know them as well. By fellowshipping with other families in the church, you'll start to feel like you belong, and when you arrive at church, you'll feel like you're with your friends!

Always involve your kids. Are you getting sick of me saying that yet? If you want to encourage your kids to become a part of the church, they must have a part in what you do. Don't make church something separate that you and your husband do while the kids just happen to tag along. Encourage your kids to cross generational borders. It will help them break out of their comfort zones. Have you ever observed your kids at church? I know my kids like to find their friends and talk to them, and that's fine, but I like to challenge my kids to talk to somebody they wouldn't normally talk to. Teach them to seek out someone who's in a different generation than they are and start to form a relationship. Talk to them ahead of time about some questions they could ask to start a conversation with somebody they don't know and then make sure you ask them about their conversations when you get home.

Encourage your kids to seek out other older Christians. They're often wise and strong in their faith and will be a good influence on your kids. There is a single man who attends our church who has captured the hearts of our children. When they see him walking in, they get excited and meet him at the door. They're always excited to catch up on each other's weeks, and after the service, they talk about fishing and hunting. They have developed quite the relationship!

Don't Forget About the Shut-ins

Another great way for you to make church a priority is by visiting the shut-ins. There are many senior Saints who have served God faithfully their whole lives and are now unable to leave their homes. Find out what needs they have and take your kids to their homes to help. I can guarantee there are lawns to be mowed and leaves to be raked. Sometimes, just a plain, old-fashioned visit is enough to cheer up a lonely shut-in.

There was a lady in the church my husband pastored several years ago who loved our kids very much. We would take them over to help with whatever she needed, and she would always be excited to serve them juice and cookies. She made sure to have them on hand when our kids came, and she loved seeing little kids playing in her house. She spent countless hours remembering when she raised her own kids and even her grandkids. The blessing of spending time with her always fell more on us. We thought we were there to cheer her up, but she always made us feel like the special ones. As you can see, it's all about relationships in the church. The more connected you are to the people in your church; the more you'll feel like church is a priority to you.

Friendships in the Church

Encourage your kids to make friends with the other kids in your church. Include them in your birthday parties and outings. If you're going to do a special outing with your family, don't hesitate to invite one of the kids from church. Plant strong and deep roots in your church home. Make your kids long to be there.

Be Involved

In order to make church a priority, you need to be involved. Do all you can to make sure you're more than just a pew-warmer. Anybody can sit through a church service on a Sunday morning and never really feel involved, but if you want to make church a priority, then you'll find ways to serve. Lead your kids by example. Show them what an honor it is to serve God. It's an amazing thing to be a part of a church family, and it should be seen as a privilege to serve. Find areas you're gifted in and offer your talents. Are you good with kids? Serve in the nursery. Do you have musical talent? Help with the worship team. Is hospitality your area of expertise? Offer to organize potlucks or baby showers. There is always a place to use your talents in the church; it's good for your kids to see that you're involved. It shows them you take church seriously.

In the same way it's an honor and a privilege to be a part of a church, it's an honor and privilege to serve and be faithful. If you want your kids to grow up to serve God and their local church someday, they need to see you actively participating now, but as you serve, also get your kids excited about serving in the church, as well. More importantly, make sure you're part of a church that allows kids to participate in serving, whether behind the scenes or up in front.

Our family has been blessed to be part of a church family that sees kids as an important part of the worship service. Our kids participate by taking offering, reading Scripture, playing piano specials, greeting, and running the sound booth. I'm so thankful for the opportunity for our kids to have a part in the church service *now*. It will help them to naturally ease into it when they grow up.

If your kids are saved, they have spiritual gifts as well. They need to be serving. It will get them excited about church and hopefully lead them to become active members of their church some day when they grow up. Make serving at your church the main event you look forward to all week. Talk about ways your kids can serve and see what ideas they have.

Maybe you have a child who's interested in running the soundboard. Ask the sound person if he would let your child sit with him so he could learn how to run the sound someday. You can do this in any area of service in the church; most people will be more than willing to teach your kids so that eventually they can have a break!

What Does Participating in the Church Look Like?

Naturally, I believe it's important that your family participates in church together. I'd encourage you to sit together as a family and discourage your kids from going off with their friends. Church is essential for your family, and, therefore, it's important to experience it together. Sitting together as a family will help you encourage your kids to participate in the service. That way, you can correct your kids if they're having trouble sitting quietly and listening, and you'll be able to keep a finger on what exactly is going on with your kids throughout the service. You'll also have the blessing of watching your kids learn and understand how to be a part of the worship service.

Help your kids to follow along with the singing and show them where the Scripture is during Scripture reading. Growing up, my grandma always told me, "Going to church without your Bible is like going to dinner without your fork!" Even if your kids are not old enough to read yet, have them bring a Bible and participate anyway. It's a good habit to start when they're little that, hopefully, will continue as they get older.

After the Service

After church is done, talk about the sermon with your kids and ask if they have any questions. Encourage your kids who are old enough to take notes during the service and ask them to write down anything they didn't understand. If they have a question that's too hard for you to answer, I'd encourage you to go and talk to your pastor with your child.

Also, talk to your kids about what they learned. Ask them how they will apply what they learned and see what their answer is. You can have some pretty interesting discussions with your kids about the sermon. Kids are often much deeper thinkers than we give them credit for.

A Final Word About Your Involvement

Homeschooling moms have a lot on their plate. I know because I'm one of them. It's easy to say, "I'm too busy to get involved in church," and just do nothing. If you're working hard to keep your priorities straight, then you should be able to include church as one of your top priorities.

When my husband was in seminary, he learned an acronym for the word B.U.S.Y. It means **B**eing **U**nder **S**atan's **Y**oke. If Satan can keep you busy, he can keep you from being effective. One of the first areas Christians are often willing to let go of when they're busy is their local church. I encourage you to evaluate your priorities and see if you're able to cut out something else before you stop serving in your local church.

There is usually a way you can arrange the priorities in your schedule to be able to serve at least in some small way in your church, and, hopefully, that's what you'll learn from reading this book. Now, don't get me wrong. There are times it's perfectly acceptable to say, "I'm too busy," and there are times when busyness is just an excuse.

You must evaluate your motives. Ask yourself, "Is it just that I don't want to help in the way I'm being asked and am using homeschooling as an excuse?" In other words, "Do I not have time because I'm too busy teaching my own kids, or am I really unable to serve?" Only you can search your heart to find the answer.

Homeschooling moms get asked to do a lot because everyone seems to think we have nothing but time, and, let's face it, we're good at handling a lot of things! But that doesn't give people an excuse to pile everything on us, so I want you to find a good balance. This is a good time to pray. Ask God to show you what *He* wants you to be involved in and ask Him what things He might have you drop.

Make sure you're choosing the things *you* want to be involved in and not just doing things because someone else dropped them in your lap. You'll be much more effective and serve more joyfully if you're serving in a capacity you want to. Please don't hear me say that you should only serve in an area in which you're gifted; sometimes, God might be calling you to stretch yourself. Again, you can pray and evaluate and see if that's the case.

It can be easy to get burnt out when you're a homeschooling mom. You're running a house full of kids from morning until night, oftentimes with no reprieve. Be careful not to over-commit to things you choose to help out with.

Talk to your husband and ask him for wisdom before deciding to commit to something or to quit a certain type of serving. Work hard to find the balance of how much to serve. Homeschooling moms are gifted in many ways, and churches want them! Just remember that even though homeschooling takes a lot of time and effort, attending a church and serving in it are extremely important.

The Game Plan:

- Find and attend a local church that aligns with Biblical standards. If you're already attending, great! If not, commit to finding and faithfully attending a church. Make church a priority. Are you serving? If not, evaluate what's keeping you from greater involvement. If you're actively serving, be sure to maintain a healthy balance. Don't over- or under-commit.
- Get to know someone new at church or reconnect with someone you haven't spent time with in a while. Plan to have a family from church over for dinner to fellowship and get to know them better.
- Start preparing for church on Monday. Think through the necessities you need to prepare for church. Make a checklist and post it in an area that's visible for everyone. Commit to doing at least one thing in preparation every day of the week.
- Involve the kids in preparing for Sunday. Ask them to get their clothes out on Saturday night. Make sure no one is missing a shoe or other essential. Have the kids place Bibles and Sunday School books or papers in a convenient location so they're easy to grab on your way out the door.
- Evaluate if there is anything that didn't go smoothly this Sunday and make plans to fix it for next Sunday. Each week, improve on your Sunday morning routine so that it's a day of rest and worship instead of chaos.

Chapter 5
Balancing the Priority Of Passing on Godly Character

"The greatest legacy one can pass on to one's
children and grand-children isn't money or other
material things accumulated in one's life, but rather a
legacy of character and faith."
~ Billy Graham

Other than teaching your kids the basics of salvation, character
training may be the next most important thing. When boiled
down, it's simply teaching your kids to have good character and
conduct. You know, the kind of child you can take to a restaurant
without the fear of him snorting milk up his nose, one who knows to
step aside and hold the door when someone is walking into a building,

a child who knows to speak politely when spoken to and to hold the door for a lady.

It's really just basic common courtesy, but I'd like to go even further than that and suggest it's also teaching your kids godly character. I like to look at it as a spiritual training of sorts. Basically, character training is to teach your kids to be more Christ-like, but be careful. It won't do you any good to teach your kids to have a character like Christ if he doesn't first *know* Christ and His saving grace. Of course, this will vary with the ages and stages your kids are at, but assuming your child is old enough to know and understand salvation, then please be careful.

I don't want you to miss the boat and think that if you teach your kids how to behave properly and have really good manners, you have arrived. If you have failed to teach them the gospel and have only taught them to have good character, you'll really be teaching your children to be good little hypocrites, polite ones, at best.

Your kids will learn that all they have to do is have good behavior, and everything will be fine. I want to preface this chapter by saying that character training comes as a result of a *changed* heart. Of course, you'll teach character training to your kids who don't yet know Jesus as their personal Savior, but, hopefully, this little disclaimer will help to lower your expectations a little bit.

I mentioned in Chapter One that any training begins with you. You're always going to be the best example to your kids, good or bad, because they see you every day. As a homeschooling mom, you're with your kids more than the average mom, so you have to be on top of your game! Be very careful to live out what you're teaching your kids. It can be tempting to snarl at the person who cut you off on the highway or get grouchy with the lady who's taking too long at the checkout in front of you. I know because I've been guilty of this very thing.

Please remember that your kids are watching everything you do, and they can sniff out a phony a mile away. When you're faced with an ethical decision, your kids are watching, so be sure to choose correctly. It's really difficult to teach your kids how to have Christ-like character if you don't first have it yourself. I understand we all have bad days, and when those days happen, don't be afraid to ask your kids, and God, for forgiveness.

Sometimes, it's necessary to ask them for forgiveness, and, sometimes, it's necessary to ask for forgiveness from the people around you, such as your husband, your family, or maybe a friend. You can tell them that God is working on you, too. My point is, if you want to teach godly character, you must first model it yourself. I don't want you to be discouraged; just be aware. We all have areas we need to work on. Don't give up or think you're unable to teach your kids because you feel like you have too many deficits, yourself. Grow and learn together!

There have been more times than I care to admit when I'm correcting a child for having an angry tone when speaking the same way myself. "STOP USING THAT TONE!" I've shouted in an angry huff, or I've caught myself talking to one of my kids about being patient while being frustrated myself. It's okay to admit that you sometimes mess up. You want to make sure that *you're* the first to have a teachable spirit. Your kids will sense your willingness to be changed, and they will copy you. In this case, more is caught than taught.

Kids are little sponges and they soak up *everything*. They constantly model the behavior they see. My husband's grandpa had a noticeable limp, yet he was active almost until the day he passed away. We often stopped by for a visit, and one particular day he happened to be out mowing the lawn. I didn't think much of it; Grandpa always walked with his limp.

A few days later, our oldest child, who was two at the time, came limping into our kitchen. Alarmed, I hopped up to check on him to see what the matter was.

"Logan, are you OK?" I asked.

"Yes, Mommy! I'm just walking like Grandpa Fox!"

We laughed, really hard, but there is more to that little scenario than we even knew. You see, kids are constantly watching our behavior. They study it, but, what's more, they also imitate it. Remember that what you do is being watched. Be a worthy example.

Why Should You Teach Character Training?

First, and of most importance, we should teach godly character because God tells us to. Ephesians 6:4 (NIV) says, "Fathers, don't exasperate your children; instead, bring them up in the training and instruction of the Lord." He wants us to raise kids who have godly character because it pleases Him. One of the best testimonies you can have is children who act out the faith you have taught them. We want our kids to be a good representation of God and also of us. Kids who bring honor to their parents also bring honor to God.

Teaching your kids to have godly character can do more than just be a good testimony for you. You're also setting your kids up to be great contributors to the workforce someday. Kids who have godly character and ethics grow into adults with the same traits. Think about what a wonderful place the world would be if everyone took the time to teach their kids godly character. You'll raise your kids to one day be good spouses and at the same time teach them to eventually attract a good spouse when the time is right, and if two godly people get married, they have a much greater chance of raising godly kids as well, which is also contributing to our multi-generational faith plan.

When Should You Teach Character Training?

The simple answer is *now*! I can't encourage you enough to put in the time to train now because it will be worth it in the end. Your kids will need you to teach them formally. You also need to remember that your kids won't be with you forever, and you need to seize the opportunity to teach them all you can while they're under your roof.

Character training should be done all day long on an informal basis. Remember that life is an accumulation of the little choices you make. Again, that means that all throughout the day, even though it might not seem like you're making much of a difference, you're teaching your kids to develop godly character.

Think with me for a minute about a bodybuilder. He doesn't just wake up one day with muscles strong enough to bench press 300 pounds. It takes time, effort, and choices to become a bodybuilder. He does things that contribute to that goal. He doesn't eat things he shouldn't, and he makes wise choices in the things he does eat. Then, every day, he does the work.

In the same way, you can teach your kids to develop godly character. You might not feel like you have accomplished a whole lot on a daily basis, but if you have taught your kids even one thing today, you're working toward the ultimate goal. I want you to remember it takes time to build godly character. Rome wasn't built in a day, and neither is your child's character, or yours, for that matter.

View Your Child's Sin as an Opportunity

When your kids make mistakes, and I can promise you that they will, don't look at their sin and failures as something to be feared or frustrated by. Can I ask you to begin thinking differently about your child's sin? I want you to begin to look at these obstacles as opportunities to teach your kids. When your child sins, he needs you to love him and to teach him, and most importantly, to point him to the cross.

Expect that your kids won't always have godly character and then treat them with the love, grace and discipline they need to begin developing it. Also worthy to note: despite your greatest efforts to teach your kids godly character, the fact remains, they may not develop it. Just keep trying and praying. Be faithful to keep teaching.

Now, character training should be done all day long on an informal basis, but it's also beneficial to do it formally as well. I recommend using a time during the week and putting it into your schedule. Some people like to do character training formally once a week, while others like to do it on a daily basis. Either one can easily be added to your homeschool schedule. Character training can be a natural part of your homeschool routine. That's one of the many benefits of having your kids home with you all day. You have the privilege of correcting improper behavior.

Imagine for a second what would happen if your kids were gone all day long. They would come home in need of attitude adjustments and character training. You wouldn't have all the time you do on a daily basis to teach them and train them to have godly character. This is one of my favorite parts of homeschooling.

How Exactly do you Teach Character Training?

The answer to this question is going to be as varied as your family is from mine. No two families are going to be the same, but to get you started, I'm going to give you a few practical examples of things that you can do.

1. Read the Bible together

That's as pure and simple as it comes. You could choose a character trait you want to work on with your family and begin to study it. For example, if patience is something you want to teach, you can choose to read all the topical verses that pertain to patience.

Start your homeschool day with verses that are centered on patience and then spend time talking to your kids about them. Ask questions like, "How have you been patient today?" Or, "Was there a time when you needed to be more patient?"

There are just as many bad examples in the Bible of people who made poor choices. These are great stories to read to the kids as well.

Talk about the choices some of the people in the Bible made and ask if they were good or bad. How did they display that character trait?

2. Memorize Scripture together

Memorizing Scripture is important because, in the words of the Psalmist, it helps us not to sin (Psalm 119:11). Scripture memory is something you can do together with your kids. I recommend writing out verses about certain character traits that you would like to refine and put them up around your house. It's easy to memorize something when you see it all the time.

3. Study together

Dig into Scripture with your kids and find out all there is to know about a certain character trait. Use the internet to research which verses go along with the topic. Don't be afraid to admit your deficiencies if you don't know where something is in Scripture, and don't be afraid if you don't know what something means. Figure it out together.

It's okay to grow alongside your kids and to let them know that you don't know everything there is to know. You can tell them that God is working on you, too, and you need to study Scripture as well, but try to lead them in studying the Word by being a good example.

4. Use Parables

Jesus told many great stories in order to illustrate truth. Many of the parables are useful for teaching your kids godly character traits. Take time to go through the parables and pull out all of the character traits you can find. Take time to talk about them with your kids and spend time writing things down. You can even illustrate the parables while you talk to your kids about what character traits you're learning.

5. Read Stories

Find stories that illustrate people making good, godly choices and displaying godly character. Read them together and discuss everything you see and then apply it to your kids' lives. There are many stories, both fictional and historical, that illustrate godly character traits.

A word of warning: I feel like this is a good place to mention it's also easy to corrupt good character by allowing your kids to read things, watch things, or even play things that are not godly. Make sure you know exactly what your kids are consuming. You can do a lot of godly character training, but if you don't watch out for these things, your hard work will be like a leaky hose. You won't know where all your effort is going or why you're not making any progress.

6. Use examples around you

Another great way to teach your kids godly character is to use examples around you. If you watch the news for any length of time, you'll see that there are many situations you can draw from. However, I don't recommend you watch with your kids, or, if you do that, at least use discretion.

You can also talk about people in your lives. Of course, I don't mean in a judgmental way. You'll want to be sensitive of confidential issues and never divulge other people's information, but if you know of a situation that could be used to teach your kids, by all means, use it. You don't need to tell the kids specifics about the actual situation. Just use it for your own information to pose a hypothetical situation to talk about.

Explain the scenario and then ask your kids what they think about the situation and what they may have done if they were in it. Use it to teach and ask your kids what the Bible says about this particular thing. Compare and contrast the behavior with the Bible and see what your kids would have done instead. If you don't feel comfortable using a real life example, it's okay to make up your own examples.

7. Use a formal resource

If you don't feel comfortable teaching without any resources, there are many available for you to choose from. Check online for godly character training resources and then do your best to pick the right one for your family.

8. Disciple them

In Chapter Four, we discussed the importance of discipleship; character training is a natural outflow of discipleship. If you missed my previous discussion on discipleship, then please go back and read Chapter Four – it's that important! If you're taking the time to disciple your kids, then, naturally, you'll be teaching them about character training at the same time, but it's nice to remind you how important it's to disciple your kids.

9. Circle Time

Circle time is one of the most fun things I can think of for training your kids formally.[ii] It's a specific, intentional, and formal time to have character training sessions. Think of it as a time when you can talk about anything you want to teach your kids that's not academically related. It's called Circle Time because the idea is to sit together in a circle. It doesn't have to be a circle if you prefer not to sit on the floor, but I've found the kids really like it. It's an intentional time to be together and talk about the important things you wouldn't otherwise get to in your homeschool teaching time, and character training is one of those things.

In order to do Circle Time well, you'll want to have a plan for what you're going to teach. I'd encourage you to have your older kids help out with the younger kids. They should participate as much as they can and also help out with crowd control. It's good for your little kids to see the example of their big brothers and sisters.

Make it fun and interesting and try not to go too long. I know; that's hard because there's so much to teach your kids! When we do Circle Time together as a family, we start out with prayer, and then I teach a character trait we want to work on. I explain the definition and read the Scripture that teaches the character trait. Then, I teach our kids exactly what it means.

But then it gets fun! I have my kids role-play whichever character trait I'm trying to teach. First, I have them act it out the way it's supposed to be done, and then I have them act it out the wrong way. For example, if I'm teaching about attentiveness, I might have all of the kids sit attentively while I read a passage from a book, and then I'll have all of the kids act inattentively while I read the same passage. This way, the kids can see the contrast between the behaviors and know exactly what it's I'm trying to teach and what I'm looking for when I want them to behave a certain way.

Sometimes I'll divide my kids and have half of the group act one way and the other half act in the opposite way so that the kids can see exactly what it looks like while it's being done. We usually end up laughing, and I have a great time teaching the kids. We get silly and creative, and the kids absolutely love it! We also repeat it many times, so the kids cement it into their heads. You'll be amazed at how much just going through this exercise on a weekly basis will help your kids grasp what you're trying to teach. It will make a difference in your family.

I find things are much more peaceful when I'm teaching my kids exactly what I expect. Sometimes, I lax up and forget that it's important to teach my kids character training, and then I find our house isn't as peaceful.

10. Take them to places where they need to practice

Does the thought of taking your kids out for a formal dinner make you cringe? As I mentioned earlier, sometimes it's scary to think that you have no idea what your kids might do. Hopefully, you don't have a milk snorter, but if you do, you should be able to teach him during character training time that that's not a godly character. Well, there may be a time and place for milk snorting, but teach him how to discern the difference!

I want to challenge you to take your kids out to a place they will need to practice the character training you're teaching. Make reservations for a formal dinner. If you can't afford to go for a formal dinner, you can make your dining room double as a fancy restaurant. If you want to up your game a little bit, you can invite company over to add a nice little bit of pressure.

During your formal dinner, expect good behavior. Encourage the kids to use manners and to sit still and quietly until they're called on. Praise and reward good behavior and be sure to tell them what a good job they did and that you'll soon do it again. It's always a great idea to follow it up with a nice treat.

11. Talk to your kids - A LOT!

I'm a communicator. I love to talk, and God gave me seven kids who love to talk as well! At times, that can get overwhelming, but I'm thankful my kids love to converse because talking with them gives me a chance to see their hearts.

I'd encourage you to talk to your kids as much as you can. Spend time communicating with them and let them know what you expect. By talking with your kids, you can begin to see which areas of character they might need a little help with.

Recently, after recognizing an area he needed work in, one of my sons came to my husband and me and asked if we could help him learn patience. He asked us to help guide him through Scripture so he could work on a character trait he knew needed attention. Don't think that your kids don't want to learn. More than likely, they have the desire to grow in their character. They just might not know how.

Teach them what they did wrong when they have messed up. Teach them why what they did doesn't line up with the Bible and how they can do things differently next time. However, I want to encourage you to first build a relationship of communication so that you have the foundation laid. Your kids will be much more inclined to talk to you about problems that come up if you have spent time talking to them about interests they have.

While all of your kids need time to talk to you, it's especially important for your older kids. They need to be able to connect with you on a heart level. Conversation is just the way to do that. Your time is one of the most valuable assets you can give to your kids, and talking is the icing on the cake.

12. Ethics questions

As your kids grow, your character training will change. We love to use ethics questions with our older kids to teach them right responses. It's fun to ask them questions to see what their response would be in a certain situation. One question you could ask is, "Would it be okay to lie to get a friend out of trouble?" I'm not going to tell you the answer to this question, but discuss it with your kids and see what they say!

You can fit in the appropriate character traits as you talk and remind him to think and act like a Christian. This will prepare him for some of the situations he will likely see when he gets out into the real world.

13. Expect good behavior

Many times, I've heard parents say, "Oh, boys will be boys," or, "You know my son, you just can't tell him what to do," or, my favorite, "Wait till they become teenagers!"

How can we expect our kids to develop and display godly character if we have such low expectations? Don't fall into the trap of making excuses for your kids. Have you ever found yourself saying, "She's just shy," when someone talks to your daughter, and she won't make eye contact? Teach your daughter that when a person talks to her, she can exercise godly character by looking them in the eye with a smile and respond when she's spoken to. You can even practice this in Circle Time. Just please, please, please, don't excuse bad behavior.

Some Helpful Phrases We Like in Our House

These are some phrases we have always said to our kids to help build godly character. I wanted to share them with you:

"God always knows and sees everything you do." This phrase will help give your kids an awareness of God and it helps them to obey because God is worthy and not just due to the fear of getting caught. Give your kids a healthy awareness of God and let them know that God is everywhere and He *sees* what they do. Remind your kids to please God even when they think no one is looking. God always knows.

"Be sure that your sin will find you out." We may not ever know what our kids do, but God does. As I said above, God knows everything, and He will deal with it one day. We have explained to our kids that they may not experience the consequences of their sin right now, but, eventually, God will deal with it.

"Sin is far-reaching." We teach our kids that when they sin, it affects more than just them. We give examples and help them to see everyone who's affected as a result of their choices.

"Always leave things better than you found them." Thanks to my mom and her teaching, I can *never* leave my hotel room messy! I have to make the bed! Since my mom did such a good job instilling it in me, I still live by that motto today, and, in turn, I'm teaching my kids the same godly character trait.

They Will Never be Perfect

Don't be afraid of your kids' sins or failures. When your kids make mistakes, and I promise you they will, I don't want you to look at their sins and failures as something to be feared or frustrated by. Can I ask you to begin thinking differently about your child's sin? I want you to begin to look at these obstacles as opportunities to teach him. When your child sins, he needs you to love him and to teach him, and, *most importantly*, to point him to the cross.

Expect that your kids won't always have godly character, and then treat them with the love, grace, and discipline they need to begin to develop it. As frustrating as their disobedient moments are, they're really just little opportunities to give grace and the gospel to your kids. When your kids get caught doing something sinful, encourage them that God, in his goodness, allowed them to get caught so they wouldn't continue on the path they were on. Of course, this means that you need to correct them and discipline them accordingly, but it will help them to see that failure isn't something that needs to ruin their life.

Just like a car needs constant correction in order to stay on the road, so our kids need to be constantly steered on the straight and narrow path. It's okay to teach your kids they're heading in the wrong direction sometimes. Teaching them godly character traits will act as a compass for them to know when they're getting off course. If you work hard at it, little kids who don't know much about godly character will grow into big kids with great godly character. It just takes time and training.

The Game Plan:

- Brainstorm ideas in which you can formally and informally train your kids to have godly character. Think of actionable ways to practice and remember that training kids is a process. Be patient!
- Develop a plan for Circle Time. Start finding resources for the things you would like to teach your kids. Find books that teach character. Commit time to doing Circle Time on a regular basis.
- Find ethics questions to discuss with your children. This is a form of character training for your children who are older. Spend time listening to your kids and discussing different viewpoints. Use Scripture to back up anything you say.
- Think of some key phrases you would like to teach in your house. Write them on paper or make printable signs to hang up around your house. Connect the phrases with the godly character you're trying to teach. Be sure to live it out yourself.
- The next time your child sins, think of it as a teachable moment rather than a time to be angry and upset. Use the opportunity to bring them back to the gospel and their need for a Savior. Don't be alarmed; rather, offer love and acceptance. Then gently teach him or her how to get back on the right track.

Chapter 6
Balancing the Priority Of Enjoying your Family

"Each day we make deposits in the memory banks of
our children."

~ Chuck Swindoll

One of my favorite parts of being a mom is being part of a family. I
absolutely love the atmosphere of family and everything that
surrounds it. There's something secure about knowing you're part of a
family unit that loves each other and enjoys being together. Of course,
not every minute of the day is rosy, but in the end, we all love each
other and know we have a place to belong.

Sometimes, family can be put on the back burner instead of other seemingly more important activities we think are a high priority. As a homeschooling mom, it's very important that you make time for your family. You need to make sure that being together is one of your top priorities and that you're translating that all the way down to the youngest member of your family. It's pretty special to be a part of a family, and you want your kids to know and appreciate that.

Core Family Values

Have you even taken time to think about exactly who your family is? Do you know what you believe as a family? I'm not just talking about your doctrinal issues or the way you view Scripture. I mean, what drives your family, and how do you determine which things will make the cut and be allowed into your home? What will you let your kids do on a daily basis? One of the most important and essential things you can do is write down core family values. You may be wondering why it's so important. Primarily, having core family values keeps your family at the center of your priorities, after God, of course.

I encourage you to sit down with your husband and talk through the goals you have as you raise your kids. Base your core family values on Scripture so you know your family is standing rock solidly on the Word of God. Ask yourselves, "What are our end goals?" When you think about how you want your kids to end up, how do you envision them?

Please keep in mind that this isn't a guarantee to raise your kids perfectly or that they will absolutely turn out the way you have in mind, but it's a great starting place. If you were to build a house, the first step would be to lay out a blueprint and have an idea in your head of what you want it look like when it's finished. The same is true for your kids. You want a general idea of what your kids will turn out to be like. Ask yourself questions like:

- Is the Bible central to all we believe?
- How will we handle failures?
- Do these activities point us to Christ?
- Will it bring us closer as a family?
- How will it affect our family as a whole?
- How will we handle outside influences?
- Will we allow sleepovers?
- How do we feel about electronics?

These are just a few of the questions my husband Ben and I have considered, and you might have other questions you can think of as well. Write all of your questions down and then prayerfully consider them as a couple. I encourage you to think of as many questions as you can. The more specific you can be, the better. When you're finished, print out your family's core values and hang them somewhere prominent.

Once you know your values, it will be much easier to measure your activities by them. Think of your core family values as a compass to direct your family and its decisions. It stands as a measurement to help you figure out the course and direction you want to take in parenting your kids. It also acts as a filter for sorting out which things to participate in and which things are better off let go.

It's a good idea to go over your core family values with your kids so they know exactly what your family stands for. That way, the next time an opportunity comes up for someone in your family, whether it be sports or a sleepover at a friend's house, you'll know exactly what you believe and stand for, and so will your kids.

Remember that each family has their own values, and your values are not better or worse than anyone else's. If you keep that perspective, it'll help keep you from becoming judgmental when you find that other families allow things you don't.

When I was growing up, everybody in the sixth grade class had spandex shorts, and I desperately wanted a pair. They were so cool, and I knew that if I had a pair, I'd be right in style. Everybody I knew had a pair of spandex shorts except me! I remember begging my mom over and over to *puh-lease* let me have a pair of spandex shorts. My mom's answer was always simple: "Others may; we don't."

As Ben and I raise our children, we have adopted the same motto. It's a catchy phrase to tell our kids when they wonder why they can't do something just because someone else is. It's important to teach your kids that not everyone has the same values, and that's okay. It doesn't make us better or worse than anyone else.

Spending Time Together

There are a million and one things threatening to take your family's time on a daily basis. It's ironic how even sitting together at the family dinner table is less of a norm anymore. The classic American family has kids going in all directions to every event imaginable and every club in between. Entire families spend days never seeing each other and it happens in homeschooling families as well.

As a homeschooling mom who wants to keep family as one of her top priorities, you're going to have to work hard to keep family first. It's okay to say "No" to more activities than not. You don't have to be a part of everything.

A few years ago, our kids were invited to be a part of our local homeschool basketball team. My husband and I considered it carefully before deciding it would be okay for them to participate. Now, here's the deal: I absolutely love how our basketball team is set up. Our kids practice at the same time, and they also play their games on the same nights, for the most part.

It makes such a difference to have our kids participating in the same thing together. The kids encourage each other and cheer each other on during games, and they're excited to see each other play. Then, they talk about the games all the way home and into the next day. It's sweet to see the friendship it brings between siblings.

This wouldn't be possible if every one of our seven kids had a different activity that pulled us all in different directions each night of the week. From a parent's perspective, that's overwhelming. There's no way I can be in seven places at once! It's simply not conducive to raising your family for the Lord if you never see each other and never have time to talk. Building relationships with your kids takes time, and you can't put in the time if you're never home together.

Please think long and hard before letting your kids participate in activities. Carefully consider the event at hand and filter it through your core family values. Obviously, no two families are the same, and you can't guarantee that all of your kids will like one sport like mine do, but the point is that you should make sure the activity you're considering fits into your core family values before you allow your kids to participate. Be really careful not to fall into the trap of doing everything. There will always be more activities than time to do them.

However, once you decide on an activity and approve it, dive in! Be excited about your kids and the opportunity they have to do something. Don't make them feel guilty for taking time out of the family schedule. If you have approved it, go with it! Be all in!

Family Worship and Prayer

We have already gone over the basics of Family Worship together, but it's worth mentioning that this is one of my favorite activities we do together as a family. If you missed the details and specifics of how family worship works, I encourage you to back and read Chapter One.

The family that prays together stays together. So, pray about everything! We have already talked about the importance of prayer, but it's worth reminding you that prayer is an important part of making your family a priority.

Make Family Times Special

When I think about special family times, for some reason, *The Waltons* comes to my mind. Even though I wasn't old enough to see the original show aired on network TV, I used to love staying home sick from school so I could watch *The Waltons*. It seemed like no matter what was going on, the whole brood of kids was always together, encouraging each other as they did a project or got into trouble! They had a strong family unit that loved and supported each other, and it was evident in the way they enjoyed each other's company.

When I think of that show, I think of people smiling and teasing each other playfully throughout each episode, and if you've seen it, you probably remember the ending scene of every episode as they all said goodnight to each other.

"Goodnight, John Boy."

"Goodnight, Mary Ellen."

That strong family bond comes through spending time together. Do your best to make family time special. You only have so much time with your kids before they will be grown and gone, so it's important to make sure you're spending special time together as a family now. As I said earlier in the chapter, there are a million and one things you could do with your time, but for some reason, family time is one of the first things to be put on the back burner. Be intentional about making family time special.

Holidays, Birthdays, and Traditions, Oh So Special

Of course, holidays should be special. It's fun to develop traditions you know will be a part of your family for years to come. Do you enjoy baking cookies for Christmas? Does everyone in your house like to dress up in green for St. Patrick's Day? Find or make special traditions you can do as a family to make holidays special.

Unfortunately, it seems like Christmases or holidays seem to come at a time when our bank account is the lowest. Add kids to the mix, and it can be hard to stay consistent with much. Naturally, I have a vision in my head of something I'd like to happen. Making it happen is another story, and although my intentions are good, they don't make memories.

In my head, I envision matching pajamas for all the kids, hand-sewn by me in a beautiful, red flannel. There's an early breakfast buffet served before everyone opens their gifts, which are color-coordinated with bows on top of each present. I can think things up; I just seem to be bad at actually making the tradition happen, and you know what? It hasn't damaged any of my kids. They're okay with having a mom who's not the greatest at making cut-out cookies every year in time for Christmas. Although, sometimes, I manage to make them in time for Easter!

It seems like every year, we try something new and say we're going to start a tradition. Then, for whatever reason, I'm never able to carry it through the next year. Several years ago, just to be funny, my husband said, "Let's start a tradition of making one *new* tradition every year!" Everyone laughed and thought it was so funny, but you know what, it's exactly what we did! Now, our tradition is to think of a new tradition every year, and we have fun doing it!

Without even mentioning it, one of our kids always says, "We can't forget to make our new tradition!" It's silly, but it's *our* silly, and you need to find something your family can look forward to each year. Just do something that will make your family tradition special, and if you're good at making traditions, and you do really well with following through each year, you have my highest compliments!

Birthdays are another special time to make very important. We make sure to schedule a birthday party when everyone from our immediate family can be there before planning around friends' calendars. It's important for family to be together to celebrate the honored person. I love to see that, as our kids plan their birthday parties, they check each other's schedules to make sure no one will be missing from the party.

Even though I'm not good at traditions, the very first tradition we made as new parents is one tradition that actually stuck with us throughout the years. Before every birthday party officially starts, we gather our family and whoever may be present at the time (aunts, uncles or grandparents, for example), and we pray with the honored birthday child. My husband prays a blessing over our son or daughter and asks God to bless the following year and draw this child nearer to Him each day. He also prays that God will help draw them to Salvation if they don't yet know Him as their Savior. This gives us an intimate moment with the birthday boy or girl before all the fun and festivities begin. Little things like this are just ways you can make your family time special. Get creative and think of some things that might work with your family and then don't be afraid to implement them.

Fox Family Olympics

Another fun thing we started is the Fox Family Olympics. I wish I could tell you we do it every year at the same time, but I already confessed how bad I'm at keeping traditions. Nevertheless, we have a really fun time! We start out by thinking and talking about which events we would like to have. We consider each child's ideas and put the events that made the cut across the top of a blank piece of paper. It's a good idea to have events that each child can participate in, so that means if you have varying skill levels and ages, you'll need varying events. Then, we make a big deal about having the Official Olympic Sign Up a few days before the games begin.

It's fun to hear the kids talk to each other throughout the week as they wait for the big day to approach. Some of our kids have even gotten into training! We have done events like ball kicking, relay races, basketball tournaments, ping pong tournaments, chess tournaments, and "javelin" throwing. These are some ideas of what we like to do, but you can make the events be anything your family enjoys.

On the day of the games, we usually make a snack like Olympic Popcorn (popcorn with white chocolate and red and blue sprinkles) or pretzels shaped into rings. We've even done Fruit Loops for the Olympic rings. Pinterest has many good ideas for Olympic snacks.

Then, the fun begins. Each child chooses which country they would like to represent, and they introduce themselves. You can imagine how fun that is! The kids like to pretend they're talking in a different accent, and we pretend to sing a national anthem from that country. We encourage them to learn fun facts about each of their countries so they can best represent them. It's a great opportunity to teach cultural awareness while having a fun time doing it.

Then, as they participate in the games, we make sure that everyone gets cheered for. This is a good time for us to talk about being a good winner and a gracious loser. We encourage each other, but we also have friendly competition throughout the day. We tells our kids, "Be a good winner and a gracious loser. Don't gloat and don't pout." We just won't allow it. At the end of the Fox Family Olympics, we announce the winner and have something special for dinner. Encourage each of your kids to participate, no matter how old they are. Not everyone will be able to participate in every activity, so this is a good time to teach them about cheering each other on and waiting patiently.

Be Creative

These are some ways our family has made spending together special. You can use these or other ideas to make sure you spend time together as a family. Get creative! Dream up and brainstorm ideas of your own. You could do a game night or bake together. Ask your kids if they would like to do a craft together or play a sport like basketball, soccer, or baseball. I know some families who have an intense game of football together on Thanksgiving Day. The tradition has even continued after their kids have grown and married and has become a friendly family competition with each of their extended families.

Ask your kids what they would like to do to spend time together as a family. I know our kids can come up with some pretty fun ideas, and you'll never regret spending too much time with your kids. It's true that they grow up fast, and you'll want to take advantage of the time you have. Spending time together with your kids means a lot to them. Later, it may even mean keeping them out of trouble.

Develop Lasting Relationships with Each Member of the Family

If you're not intentional about spending time together as a family, you can quickly become a bunch of strangers living under one roof, and sometimes, strangers don't like each other. Why? Because they don't *know* each other! It's important to encourage your kids to spend time together. Not every day can be a family day, and the things we discussed earlier are more for special occasions, but you need to spend *some* time together every day.

There are so many things pulling at your time, and too many families have kids going in every direction. Sports practices, friends, activities with church - it seems like there is always something vying for your kids' attention, and in order for your family to become a priority, your kids must spend time together. I've really enjoyed watching the relationships develop between each one of my kids, from the oldest to the youngest. We have always made sure our kids know they will always have each other and that their relationships run deep.

We make it a point not to let our kids' friends come before each other. I realize that your kids will sometimes need to spend time apart, but if you find that there is a divisive friend who consistently drives a wedge between two of your kids, you need to make sure they sever the relationship with that friend. One good way for your kids to be driven toward family is to look for other families who are also serious about keeping their family together and then make it a priority to get together with them.

When I was growing up, I only had one sister, and she was five years younger than me. We never really got to do a lot together because our interests were always so different due to our age gap. We were never into the same thing at the same time. I think that's where my love for a large family began to grow. I wanted to make sure my kids had siblings they could play with and develop relationships with, so I've made it my passion to make sure my kids grow up to be best friends.

Starting at a very young age, I was sure to tell them they have friends in their own house they can play with at any time. Ben and I have made it a point to teach them that friendships outside the home will change and fade, but they will always have each other. Make it a point to give your kids a vision for the future of their relationships. Let them know that someday, you'll likely be gone, but they will still have each other. Most importantly, teach your kids to marry spouses who will enhance their relationship with the rest of the family. That starts right now with teaching them how to have friendships that enhance their relationships inside the family.

We have been careful to nurture the relationships between our kids. Their friendships need to be cultivated. Like I said earlier, that comes from spending time together on a daily basis. In order to do this, I arrange play times together between each of my kids. Not only does this help me, since I know the kids are occupied when I have things to do, it also helps strengthen their sibling bond. Sometimes, I direct which kids play with which to ensure that each of my kids plays together and works on developing a relationship with each other. Other times, I let them decide who will play together.

Now that I have kids who are old enough to go off on their own, I make sure they don't get too busy to do things together, still. I don't let them fill their schedules so full that they can't find time to be with the family, but I don't usually have to make them do that. Most of the time, our kids are asking if their siblings can come along when they spend time with their friends.

Both my in-laws and my grandma have taken turns taking our kids out for supper. They always do a birthday meal for the kids. Each time, they're allowed to invite a friend, and, almost every time, they have decided to take one of their siblings. That makes my mommy heart sing!

Develop and Maintain Open Communication

Any relationship needs to have good communication in order for it to be solid. Teach your kids how to have good communication with each other. Don't allow them to fall into the world's standards of communication, which are either broken and messed up, or nonexistent. Help them to understand that when they have a problem with each other, they need to work it out - and quickly! I've been a stickler about tattling in my house. Nothing bothers me more than standing in the kitchen cooking dinner and refereeing a fight that's going on in the living room.

When my kids come to me to tattle, I ask, "Have you tried to work it out with your brother or sister?" I want them to try working it out themselves from a Biblical perspective. Matthew 18:5-17 describes it very well, and I highly recommend taking the time to teach your kids how to use it. Although this passage is speaking about dealing with sin in the church, I believe it sets a good example for how to work out a problem between siblings.

The first thing you need to teach your kids is to go to the person they're having a problem with and talk to them. More often than not, the problem never goes any further, but if the person won't listen, then it's okay to take someone else along. In that case, we encourage our kids to ask one of their siblings to help. I'm amazed at how often problems get resolved, and I never even have to step in. I stand in the kitchen and listen intently as my kids work it out. It's amazing!

If they can't work out the problem after talking it through with another person involved, then they're free to come to me in a non-tattling, non-whiny manner. I'll help them if I need to, but as I said earlier, I don't like to be a referee!

When you teach your kids how to resolve conflict between each other as children, you'll teach them how to handle conflict as an adult, and I can guarantee beyond a shadow of a doubt that they will encounter conflict at some time in their lives. Give them the tools now for how to deal with interpersonal relationships, and they will thank you later!

Keep an Eye on Friendships

Another thing to watch out for when developing a strong family relationship is the friendships that your kids have. Be sure you don't just know who your kids' friends *are*, but that you get to know them personally. 1 Corinthians 15:33 (NIV) says, "Don't be misled. Bad company corrupts good character;" I believe the reverse is true, also: good company encourages good character.

If your kids are hanging out with godly kids who have morals similar to yours, they will encourage each other to grow in their faith, but keep a close watch on who your kids are spending time with. We have made sure to keep our home open and let our kids have their friends over. We want to get to know our kids' friends. Not only is it helpful, but we enjoy the kids our children have developed friendships with. We've also allowed our kids to go to their friends' homes because we know who they are and know that the influences on our kids are good.

One of the neat things I've found while being a homeschool family is that, typically when our kids have friends over, everyone is involved together. I know it's important for kids to feel like they can spend time one-on-one with their friends, but resist the urge to let friendships outside the house get exclusive.

In other words, let *all* your kids feel involved in the friendship. Don't let exclusive friendships overtake family friendships. We have a saying in our house, "There's always room for one more," and on that note, we usually let our kids spend time playing a game together as a group and then giving individual time for a friend and the child he has come to visit, just on a more limited basis. When one of our kids has a friend over, all of our kids get excited to spend time together. No one goes to their room with a friend and shuts the door. Everyone feels included.

Finally, teach your kids to stand up for each other so they know they will always have an advocate. Your kids need to know their family has their backs. I've seen too many families allow bullying to take place right inside the home. If you want to make a strong family unit, please make sure your kids know to stand up for each other.

Keep Talking to your Kids

When I was growing up, I talked a lot. Okay, I still do! I used to love spending time talking to my mom and my grandma. I always thought it was funny when I heard my friends say they couldn't talk to their parents. It never occurred to me that somebody wouldn't *want* to talk to their parents. We talked about everything, and no question was off-limits. I remember sitting at my grandma's kitchen table while she cooked. She would give me a small kitchen job to do while I chattered away, talking about all the things that were important to me. She talked to me and as a result of those conversations, I knew I was loved. I still sit in the same spot in my grandma's kitchen, holding my babies, and now *they* talk to her. (And I still do, too!)

In our house, we have worked hard to keep the lines of communication open as well. I enjoy the conversation that comes through my kitchen. Many times, I'm busy cooking, and one of my kids comes in to talk to me about whatever's on their mind. It's funny how the tables are now turned, and I'm the one cooking, and my kids are the ones talking.

When you talk to your kids, you let them know you love them by being interested in what's happening in their lives. You show them that being part of a family is a special thing. Trust me when I say that you'll want to keep the lines of communication open, and that starts right now. There *will* be a time when you need to talk to your kids about something, I guarantee it. The more sensitive the nature, the more difficult it can be, but if you work hard now to keep talking to them, then when that time comes, it will be much easier to talk to your kids, and on the contrary, when they have a problem, they know they can come talk to you.

You Can Be Friends with Your Kids

Have you ever thought about being friends with your kids? As they grow up, you'll have the opportunity to develop a friendship with them. It's kind of funny to think about right now, but I guarantee you if you take the time to make them a priority and talk to them a lot, you'll develop a lifelong friendship, and that starts by making family a priority.

A Safe Place to Fall

Your family needs to be a safe haven where your kids can be themselves. In our house, we're silly and goofy and crazy and do things no one else sees us do. We have taught our kids that what happens in the home stays in the home. We want our kids to feel it's safe for them to be themselves within our family environment, that if they act silly or make a mistake, the family is here to support them, so we have taught them they're not allowed to post on social media or talk to their friends about our family matters.

Your kids will undoubtedly make mistakes. There will be times you feel disappointed, discouraged, frustrated and angry, but your family needs to be the one place your kids feel safe. They need to know that at the end of the day, no matter how much they have failed, you still love them. They need to know that grace, love, and forgiveness abound and that they can count on their family to love them through the aches and pains of growing up.

There *will* be times where you have to extend grace and love. As your kids mature, they will test the limits and boundaries you have placed. That's part of learning to hold on to a faith that will one day become their own, so when your kids make mistakes, don't be afraid or discouraged. Know that you're there to provide a safe place for them to fall, a place where you can point them to Christ and His finished work on the cross. Let them know they're loved, and nothing they can do will change that. Tell and show them often. There is no better place to do that than at home with your family.

The Game Plan:

- Using the questions listed at the beginning of the chapter, develop your Core Family Values together with your husband. Take time to go over them as a family, explaining why you feel they're important. Post them in a visible place and refer to them often.
- Choose something special to do together as a family and commit to doing it. Ask for input from your kids and take a family vote. Be sure to include activities for all ages.
- Identify your family traditions and talk about why they're special to your family. If you don't have any, make one up, and then commit to practicing your traditions. Talk about why traditions are a neat part of being a family.
- Evaluate your kids' friendships. Do you know your kids' friends? If not, get to know them. If you already do, plan a time when you can spend time together with your kids and their friends. Are there any friendships that need to be reconsidered?
- Spend time talking to your kids about their mistakes. Share about a time you made a mistake and what your response was to it. Let your kids know you love them no matter what and that you're always there for them when they do fail.

Chapter 7
Balancing the Priority Of Being the Keeper of Your Home

"I believe that a godly home is a foretaste of heaven. Our homes, imperfect as they are, must be a haven from the chaos outside. They should be a reflection of our eternal home, where troubled souls find peace, weary hearts find rest, hungry bodies find refreshment, lonely pilgrims find communion, and wounded spirits find compassion."
~ Jani Ortlund

My home is my happy place, and there's nowhere else I'd rather be. I take the job of keeper of the home seriously, and I love having an area to manage. As a homeschooling mom, one of your top priorities is to be the keeper of the home, and it's a big responsibility. Did you know this task is so important God even makes mention of it in the Bible? Titus 2:5 (ESV) says, "to be self-controlled, pure, working at home, kind, and submissive to their own husbands, that the word of God may not be reviled." God sees your responsibility as a keeper of the home as a very noble calling.

It's a Joy, Privilege, and Responsibility

The trouble is, housework is hard, and, sometimes, it gets overwhelming to keep up with everything involved in managing a house while you're also trying to homeschool. I think it helps to have a shift of mindset because anything you view as work is going to feel mundane.

How do you view your house? Do you see it as a privilege? When I'm tempted to complain about laundry, dishes or cleaning yet another toilet, which seems like a daily occurrence in our household of nine people, I change my thinking. I think about the fact that there are many people who would *love* to have a house to live in. In the US alone, the amount of people who are homeless is shocking. Try shifting your mindset a little bit and start seeing your home as a privilege and the people in your house as an opportunity to serve and glorify God.

It really is a joy to serve your family as the keeper of the home. However, the world wants you to believe it's anything but a joy. In fact, many times, a woman is looked down upon or ridiculed if she's *just* a stay-at-home mom, but in fact, God says otherwise. Proverbs 31:10-31 (NIV) says,

> Her husband has full confidence in her
> and lacks nothing of value.
> She brings him good, not harm,
> all the days of her life.
> She selects wool and flax
> and works with eager hands.
> She's like the merchant ships,
> bringing her food from afar.
> She gets up while it's still night;
> she provides food for her family
> and portions for her female servants.
> She considers a field and buys it;
> out of her earnings she plants a vineyard.

She sets about her work vigorously;
her arms are strong for her tasks.
She sees that her trading is profitable,
and her lamp doesn't go out at night.
In her hand she holds the distaff
and grasps the spindle with her fingers.
She opens her arms to the poor
and extends her hands to the needy.
When it snows, she has no fear for her household;
for all of them are clothed in scarlet.
She makes coverings for her bed;
she's clothed in fine linen and purple.
Her husband is respected at the city gate,
where he takes his seat among the elders of the land.
She makes linen garments and sells them,
and supplies the merchants with sashes.
She's clothed with strength and dignity;
she can laugh at the days to come.
She speaks with wisdom,
and faithful instruction is on her tongue.
She watches over the affairs of her household
and doesn't eat the bread of idleness.
Her children arise and call her blessed;
her husband also, and he praises her:
"Many women do noble things,
but you surpass them all."
Charm is deceptive, and beauty is fleeting;
but a woman who fears the Lord is to be praised.
Honor her for all that her hands have done,
and let her works bring her praise at the city gate."

You can see the testimony of the woman mentioned here and the way she viewed her home. Verse 17 says, "She sets about her work vigorously; her arms are strong for her tasks." Her attitude was hardworking and one of contentment. Start to see your house as a place you can joyfully serve, and you can overcome the temptation of seeing your home as a burden, but you must start by seeing your role as the keeper of the home from a biblical perspective. Taking care of your home will become a priority and a pleasure when you see it through God's eyes.

Your Friends Can Make All the Difference

One of the best ways to value your position is to surround yourself with friends who see it the same way. There is an old adage that says, "Misery loves company," and I believe it. If you hang out with people who see housework, dishes, laundry, and taking care of their family as nothing but a drag, the chances are you'll begin to feel the same way. On the other hand, if you find friends who view staying at home as an awesome privilege, you'll likely appreciate your position more.

Avoid the Two Cs: Complaining and Comparison

Please don't fall into the trap of complaining. This can be done in your heart or out loud. I'm ashamed to admit there are days I grumble quietly to myself about all the responsibilities involved in taking care of my house. I may never say anything out loud to anyone, but God knows my heart (Psalm 44:21), and I'm guilty of not always doing things with a happy heart. It's funny because I'm really quick to tell my kids to do everything without grumbling or complaining (Philippians 2:14), but I know for certain I don't always do that well myself.

It's also very important that you avoid the comparison trap. There's no greater and quicker way to become discontent than to compare yourself with others, and the first place to start comparing what you have with what you wish you had is Pinterest. I love Pinterest an awful lot. I can spend hours pinning beautiful pins of matching decor and flower centerpieces for my dining room table. I dream about what it would be like to have a house decked out in shabby chic furniture with nothing out of place. My dream home would have perfectly framed pictures of perfectly clean kids smiling their perfect smiles on a perfectly constructed shiplap wall.

Suddenly, I look up from my Pinterest board and see toys in the middle of the floor, my three-year-old with spaghetti stains on his cheeks, couch cushions that need to be straightened yet again, and dust bunnies hiding out under the coffee table. What happens to my heart when I see that comparison? The house I was content to live in with the people I love now seems anything but acceptable. A tiny seed of discontentment starts to take root in my heart without my even knowing it. Interestingly enough, when I go to wash my dishes, I notice there's a chip out of the corner of my coffee mug, and my silverware doesn't all match. Now, I start to complain a little bit in my heart because things aren't perfect.

My friend, I urge you to use Pinterest and other forms of social media carefully. The things you see constructed on those walls are not reality. I have yet to see a real person live in an *all* white house with kids that never have an ounce of dirt on them. When you see pins on Pinterest, you're only seeing part of the picture. You may not realize it, but most of what you're seeing is staged, and you don't know how long it took the person taking the picture to make it look so perfect.

On the other hand, avoid the comparison trap of pride by making yourself feel better than anyone else. Maybe you *have* been able to achieve a Pinterest life, and if you have, that's amazing, but avoid comparing yourself to those who haven't. Don't allow pride to seep in and make you feel like you're any better than anyone else. Be careful to keep a humble spirit and don't compare your house to anyone else's, good or bad. The heart of the matter is to be content with what you have.

If you Struggle, Ask God for Help

I know the reality is that, somewhere along the line, you'll struggle with being a keeper of your house. Let's face it: homeschooling, being a good wife, and a good mom, are already a lot of things to handle without the added responsibility of keeping up with your house. Believe me; there have been times I've wished I could afford a maid, so it's not uncommon for you to feel like you struggle with keeping up with your house. We have all been there.

It's hard to find time, energy, and, sometimes even the desire to keep up with your house, and if you have little kids running around, time and time again, you get one mess taken care of at the sacrifice of another. I totally understand that. It can be overwhelming to juggle everything on your plate. Hopefully, by reading this book, you're starting to feel a little bit better about everything you have to handle. It's my prayer that this book will help you balance your priorities.

When you Feel Like Giving Up

Before you do anything else, read Scripture. There are many verses that will show you God really cares about you and your struggle. He cares what kind of job you do in keeping up with your house, and He can offer encouragement when you're struggling the most. When I feel like I can't keep up, or like I don't even *want* to keep up, here are some of the top Scriptures I turn to (NIV):

- Isaiah 41:10: "So don't fear, for I'm with you; don't be dismayed, for I'm your God. I will strengthen you and help you; I'll uphold you with my righteous right hand."
- Galatians 6:9: "Let us not become weary in doing good, for at the proper time we will reap a harvest if we don't give up."
- Matthew 11:28: "Come to me, all you who are weary and burdened, and I'll give you rest."
- Philippians 4:13: "I can do all this through Him who gives me strength."

These are just a few verses that encourage me. Search through Scripture. Googling is a good way to find topics. In this case, Google the phrase "Bible verses for when you feel like giving up", and it will bring up good suggestions. Write them down and keep them before you; I know this kind of discouragement, and I know it doesn't just go away overnight. You need to bathe yourself in Scripture and remind yourself constantly to see your responsibilities as the keeper of the home as a privilege.

I've found it helpful to have an accountability partner. (We'll talk more about this in Chapter Eight.) If your husband is gone all day, you might not have anyone to check in with, and it would be tempting not to do anything all day. After all, the dishes aren't going anywhere! But if you can find someone who's willing to hold you accountable, you might feel more motivated to keep up with your tasks. It's a little bit harder to not get anything done knowing you'll have to tell somebody you didn't do *anything* all day, and you sat on the couch and scrolled through Facebook instead of doing laundry. You'll want to find a like-minded, stay-at-home mom who's preferably a believer. That way, you can encourage each other with Scripture, and you'll have the same core values, so it'll be easier.

I'd also like to invite you to my blog, allnaturaljoy.com. I equip moms to delight in everyday living. I know what it's like to feel overwhelmed with the daily grind, and my mission is to help moms find joy in being home. You'll also find help and encouragement for juggling homeschooling and your other responsibilities at my blog, thehomeschoolinghousewife.org

Find New Ways

If you struggle to keep up with your house, maybe you need to dedicate time to learning about it. It's not as if you got married, and you suddenly knew how to do everything that keeping up a house entails. Take time to research ways to clean a toilet quicker or make your own dish soap. Maybe you can find a way to fold clothes faster.

One time, my daughter and I learned a new technique online for folding t-shirts fast, and we had fun racing each other to see who could do it quicker. Suddenly, all the kids got involved, and we were having a race while folding t-shirts. I couldn't help but smile because, as we were enjoying racing each other, the laundry was getting folded! You might be surprised at how many things you can find that will make house cleaning quicker, easier, and ultimately more enjoyable.

Have you ever thought about taking care of your home as a hobby? I know it sounds strange. Scrubbing dishes and sweeping might not be your idea of fun, but if you can change your perspective on it, you might start to look at folding laundry as something you're excited to do. Trick yourself into thinking it's a hobby, and you never know how fun it could become. It makes me laugh to think about being excited to vacuum. Maybe I've just gone crazy, and I've been a stay-at-home mom for too long!

Most importantly, when you don't feel like doing anything, force yourself to start somewhere. Do you have a pile of laundry that's now taller than your oldest child? Are there dishes in the sink that are starting to grow mold? Is the living room carpet peppered with toys? If you're overwhelmed and have no idea where to begin, just start *somewhere*, anywhere. Pick a small task you know you can accomplish and start there.

Act Right; Feel Right

Have you ever heard the phrase, "Act right; feel right"? In other words, don't wait until you *feel* like doing your housework. If you wait until you feel like it, you might not ever do it. When I don't know what to do, the first thing I do is throw in a load of laundry. It doesn't take too long, and it starts to feel like I'm accomplishing something right away. I've found that if I start laundry, I'm much more motivated to tidy up the kitchen, which is just around the corner from the laundry room.

In order to tidy up the kitchen, I need to load the dishwasher. Once the dishes are off of the counter and into the dishwasher, I can easily wipe the kitchen counters. Now that I have the counters under control, I do a quick sweep of the kitchen floor, and the kitchen is under control. If the kitchen is under control, I might as well go to the dining room. I employ the same tactics in the dining room as I did in the kitchen, starting with something small and working up to a bigger project. As you can imagine, once the dining room is under control, the living room seems less overwhelming.

It's much easier for me to tackle the jobs from smallest to greatest, and once I start doing something, I feel more like continuing until it's done. You would be surprised how much this technique can help you feel less depressed and more motivated. Once you have your house under control, take special care to keep up with pickup and avoid allowing your house to get overwhelmingly out-of-control.

Housework Doesn't Always Come Naturally

I recognize that housework doesn't come easily to everyone, and not everyone may be a gifted homemaker, but it still needs to be one of your top priorities as a homeschooling mom. You're in your house much more than moms who are not homeschooling. As a result, it's important that you create an enjoyable environment for you and your kids.

If you're a mom who feels like housework doesn't come naturally to you, don't use it as an excuse. Instead, pray and ask God to give you the desire to make your house a priority, and, again, study Scripture to help encourage you to see your house as the blessing that it's.

It Will Make Your Husband Happy

If you make being a keeper of your home your passion, you'll bring joy to your husband. I don't know about you, but that motivates me to do a good job in taking care of my house. My husband works hard, and keeping my house clean is a great opportunity for me to serve him by showing I care.

Now, before you think I'm an old-fashioned June Cleaver, my husband *does* help me with things in the house, and I'm totally fine with that. I don't want to paint the picture that he should come home like a 1950s husband and sit in his easy chair with a newspaper, sipping a glass of fresh-squeezed lemonade while I fan in him, dressed in a pretty dress with my hair done nicely, and tend to every one of his needs, but I do want to point out that Proverbs 31:10 says that a godly wife has a husband who can trust her. That means he can trust that she will take care of things in the house while he's gone. I also understand that we live in an entirely different era, and that means both you and your husband may be working, in or out of the home. Therefore, it's even easier to blur the biblical lines of what a woman should be doing in the home.

In Titus 2:5, we see that God has given a very clear mandate for what a woman's job is. Being a keeper of the home is a God-given responsibility. Whether your husband works in or out of the home, and whether you work in addition to homeschooling or not, you still have the responsibility to keep your home in the way God commands.

How Do I Keep Up With it All?

That's an excellent question and one I have even asked out loud. "How am I supposed to do everything?" As a homeschooling mom, you have a ton of responsibilities. I could name them all, but you're probably well aware of the fact that you're juggling more things than you can count. It's easy to get overwhelmed and feel like you can never accomplish everything. I'm going to let you in on a little secret. Lean in close because I want to whisper this in your ear. YOU CAN'T!! Sorry; I yelled it! You simply can't keep up with it all. There is absolutely no way.

Now that the pressure is off, I want you to stop feeling overwhelmed. Don't allow yourself to look at the overwhelming big picture. Instead, break your day down into small chunks that are easy to take care of. When you're homeschooling, homeschool. Don't think about the dishes in the sink that need to get done. When you're dedicating time to the family and having fun, don't think about the papers you need to grade. Try to live in each moment and don't stress about the things you can't take care of. The simple truth is there will always be work to do, and there isn't enough time to do it all, so it's okay to give yourself some grace. Just don't let grace turn into laziness. As long as you live in your home, and as long as you have kids, there will always be work to do.

I really had to work hard with this concept. I pressured myself and my family to have a very nice house that was constantly in order. The problem was, while my house looked beautiful, clean, and under control, my family was miserable. It certainly wasn't worth it to have a beautiful house and kids who were frustrated by their mom. Enter my new favorite verse, Proverbs 14:4a (ESV): "Where there are no oxen, the manger is clean." In essence, if you don't have kids, your house can be beautiful and perfectly in order. Which would you prefer, a clean house and no kids, or kids, and the mess that comes with them?

Yes, kids are messy and can easily turn a clean house into a dirty one in five seconds flat, but if you train your heart to see them as the gift that they are, hopefully, you can begin to see the work they create as a blessing as well. I utter this verse to myself often during the day. It helps me remember to see my kids as a treasure.

Let's Talk About Plans

Having a plan makes a huge difference. You need a plan to keep up with all the responsibilities you have as a homeschooling mom. It's almost impossible to balance every obligation without having a basic framework of how you'll tackle everything. Just having a protocol in place starts to settle my heart and make me feel less overwhelmed. I'll give you a general framework for strategies you can implement in your household, and if you're anything like me, these plans will help. I want you to feel at ease, so let's talk about *your* plan of action!

Let's Make an Action Plan for Your House

By plan of action, I mean the basics of keeping it generally clean and in order. I can't stress enough that you *need* to involve your kids. It's so important that kids connect their actions with specific consequences. In other words, when they take out toys, they need to put them away. When they make a mess, teach them to clean it up. Even if your kids are younger, you can still involve them in parts of your housework routine. Three year olds can do a great job dusting or emptying little garbage cans (i.e. bathroom, office, etc.). You can always find some way to involve your little ones.

For quite some time, I've been making chores a part of our homeschool routine. School isn't done until the chores are, too. In order to keep our house clean on a daily basis, I use a system that works really well for our family. I went room by room and thought about each job that needed to be done. I then designed a system of chore cards, which can be purchased on my website, allnaturaljoy.com and thehomeschoolinghousewife.org. These chore cards have helped me keep the house under control with much less effort.

We also have a general pickup routine at a few different times during the day. Usually just after lunch and just before bed. If we all (including the little kids) pitch in and work together, we can straighten our house in about 15 minutes. One of my favorite phrases is, "Many hands make light work." For extra fun, sometimes I set a timer and we race to see how much we can get done before it goes off. Then when we're done we'll do something special together or have a special treat. (This isn't possible every time we need to clean up. It's fun to do occasionally.)

It's important to leave the house clean before you go to bed, even if it means taking a few extra minutes to clean up before you drag your weary-self off to bed. You'll feel much better in the morning and will be able to start the next day off on the right foot.

I've come across many homeschooling moms who feel like they can't start the school day until their house is in order. This creates a problem because school gets put off for much longer than it should while everyone is busy straightening the house. Try to make it a general rule to go to bed with the house in order. You'll be thankful you did when you wake up to an orderly house the next morning.

You'll also need to develop a weekly plan in order to keep up on the things that don't get attention every day. In the last several years, the kids and I have started doing a deep cleaning of the house on Fridays. We call it "House Blessing Day" in order to keep it more of a positive experience and less of a burden. It helps us remember our house is a gift from God.

Another reason I like a once-a week cleaning is because there will undoubtedly be days throughout the week I don't get to pick up as well as I'd like to, but I know Friday is coming, and we'll catch anything that needs to be cleaned a little deeper on that day. I do all I can to make sure we don't skip House Blessing Day!

What do We do on House Blessing Day?

The first thing we do is pray together. I find that it starts us out on the right foot, and we're much more eager to do our jobs as unto the Lord. I hand out the chore cards to each of the kids, and then we crank up some worship tunes on Spotify and get moving. Just a side note: bluegrass really makes everybody move quickly!

We actually enjoy our time cleaning the house together. If one child finishes before his siblings, I encourage him to go help someone else who might need a little company. It has been neat for me to see how the relationship between my kids has developed as a result. I smile secretly to myself as I hear one of them go to the other and ask if there's anything they can do to help.

When we're all finished, and the house is clean, we have some sort of a reward, either a special snack, a game time together, or something fun we have predetermined. This helps keep everyone motivated and feeling like working so we can reach our goal.

Please note that you can't expect perfection from your kids. You already know I like my house clean, but I had to let go of perfection as my standard. Sometimes, I have to pull one of them back into a room to show them something that could have been done a little bit better or a different way, but as long as my kids are trying their best and putting forth a real effort, I don't get too bent out of shape. A wise woman who has now since gone to be with the Lord taught me once not to worry about perfection because only God is perfect! I've tried to pass that on to my kids so they don't feel like they can never measure up, and let's just say, I'm also grateful for all their help and I want them to know that!

A Word of Caution

While a clean and orderly house is a nice thing and should be a high priority, it's not always possible that it will happen every day or even every week. Don't ditch school to make sure everything is in order. If you do, you'll have a really clean house and kids who don't know anything!

Some of My Favorite Organization Systems

Nine-hole cubicles. I use these cubicles for *everything!* If you came to my house today, you would see them in our schoolroom, our pantry, in the basement and the garage, in our kids' closets, pretty much everywhere.

In the schoolroom, they house all of our kids' curriculum and extra books. In the pantry, they're set up for slow cookers, my juicer, and any other gadgets I don't want on my countertops. In the basement, they're home to all of the kids' scarves, hats, mittens and outdoor accessories. I gave up dressers many years ago and started using cubicles to store the kids' clothes. I find it much easier for kids to keep things organized in a cubicle than a dresser.

You might even use them in a family closet. In the house we last lived in, I turned one room into a storage room for everyone's clothes. We called it the Family Closet. My husband stacked nine-hole cubicles around the entire room, and the kids' clothes were all stored in the Family Closet. It freed their bedrooms from dressers that would get cluttered and gave them much more space to play. You can use nine-hole cubicle shelves for just about anything. Just use your imagination. The sky's the limit!

Bins. Bins are my absolute favorite organization tool! They come in all shapes and sizes, and they can be stacked, stored under the bed, and used for just about anything. Currently, I have a clothing system that houses all the clothes our kids are not wearing at this time. I often joke that I could run a consignment store out of my basement. I have kids clothes organized from 0-3 months all the way up to size 16-18 in both boys and girls clothes.

A large family like ours saves a ton of money when it's time to switch over clothes for a season. First, we shop out of our basement, trying on all the clothes in a particular size for each child. We always have fun reminiscing about who wore what article of clothing last and how much of a favorite it was. It's fun for an older sibling to see a previously favorite sweatshirt on a younger child, and it's fun for the younger siblings to wear something they know their older sibling treasured.

I also use bins to store curriculum we're not currently using. As soon as we're done with the school year, I pack everything neatly into a bin and store it in the basement, safe for the next time we will need it.

I also use bins to store the kids' toys. I've been very careful to keep toys organized since my oldest child was a baby. He's now sixteen, and my three-year-old is playing with toys his big brother played with over a decade ago. Not only does it preserve toys, but it helps keep the house clean, and in a pinch, I can quickly grab a neatly labeled bin out of our playroom for my little kids to play with while I'm teaching school.

Crates. I'm ashamed to admit that if you would have asked me several years ago what system I used to organize my homeschool classroom, I'd have told you, "Nothing!" It was a disaster for everyone involved. As you can imagine, teaching school with no form of organization was complete chaos. I remember kids asking me how many pages of math to do, and I'd answer according to my mood. If I felt like having them do more work, I'd assign more, and if I felt like we should have some time off that day, I'd say to do less. Even just writing that, I see how frustrating it was for the kids.

Several years ago, I found a crate system to organize all the kids' school work. It has made such a difference in the way I'm able to keep organized while teaching school. Since the system isn't my own, I can't share it with you directly, but you can check it out at kristiclover.com.

Chores system. I mentioned earlier that I took time to organize all the kids' chores into one system. The only question I have is why I didn't do it sooner. When kids know what chores to do, the household runs like a well-oiled machine. It helps me to be a better keeper of the home. I'm able to oversee and manage the kids instead of fretfully trying to cover each responsibility myself while the kids are bored because I'm so busy working hard. I help with all the chores as I have time, but having a system in place for chores helps ensure we're all working on keeping the house under control.

My laundry system. My husband hung three baskets on the wall of our laundry room using some basic tools from the local hardware store. On each of the baskets, I labeled, "Towels", "Whites", and "Darks." When my kids bring their hampers down in the morning, a chore they have on their chore cards, they sort their laundry into each of the baskets, which means I have laundry sorted and ready to throw into the wash at any time. It's a self-sorting system. Then, each of the older kids have laundry on their chore cards. Throughout the day, they each put the clothes in the washer and dryer at appropriate times. You might say my laundry does itself!

I have also assigned kids to fold clothes and kids to put clothes away. They work together in teams, so the job isn't so overwhelming. It also makes it fun for the kids to have a partner. While one team of kids is folding clothes, the other team is bringing them to the appropriate bedrooms. I require my kids to put their clothes in their cubicles as soon as they're clean, resisting the temptation to put them on the floor or on their beds. If they're put away right away, you'll avoid washing clean laundry a second time. You can do what works in your family as far as the division of jobs goes.

I have also heard of a system called "Four by 4:00".[iii] In that system, you'll do four loads of laundry by 4:00 pm. While I don't use this system because my own system works well for me, it may be something for you to think about.

If you choose to fold clothes rather than have your kids do it, consider this sweet little activity: Pray for each person as you fold their clothing items. For example, as you fold your family's socks, pray that their feet would be ready to spread the gospel. When folding their shirts, pray that they would put on the breastplate of righteousness. For their undergarments, pray that they would gird their loins with truth. Hopefully, this will help you generate some ideas for creative ways to pray for your family, and it also makes folding clothes less of a burden and more of a ministry.

I have found many other neat systems for organizing things throughout the house on Pinterest. As I mentioned before, you can find a way to organize pretty much anything. When you organize your house, everything is more smooth and enjoyable. You won't find yourself overwhelmed by piles of laundry every day, not knowing how to dig yourself out. Your house will only need maintenance, and in the case of your absence, everything won't fall apart.

I don't do these systems perfectly, but they have definitely helped bring more joy to our household. There are many times I've failed, but when I do, I get back up and start over right where I left off. That's the beauty of an organized system. Don't be discouraged if you feel like your house is too out of control. Just work in little chunks.

You Need a Plan for Your Time

I've found it very easy to waste time as a stay-at-home mom. After all, I'm also the keeper of my own schedule. I don't have a time clock to punch, and there isn't a boss looking over my shoulder. Therefore, I really need to make sure I'm making the best use of my time *at all times*.

I mentioned finding an accountability partner earlier, and that's a great idea. If you can't or don't want to find an accountability partner, you may consider asking your husband to help you stay accountable with your time. Make sure you check in with either of them and be honest about the way you spent your day. Here are some important and helpful ways to be a good steward of your time:

Stay off social media during school hours. Resist the urge to check Facebook or email during teaching time. I'm not a person who thinks Facebook is evil - I enjoy my Facebook account and friends very much, but I know first-hand that it can suck your time quickly. It's best not to check Facebook or any other social media during school hours. If you need to, put your phone on airplane mode and don't touch it. Having said that, you do need a time when you *can* enjoy social media. It's okay to indulge in it guilt-free, but it needs to be within the confines of a time you have chosen, outside of the homeschooling day.

Don't feel bad for not answering your phone during school hours. People who don't homeschool don't always understand you're not available all day long. After all, people often wonder what you actually *do* all day, and some people might even think you don't do anything. You don't have to be available to people at all hours. I recommend setting a boundary early on. If you don't answer your phone, you won't find yourself in an hour-long conversation while your kids are hanging from the chandeliers. You also won't end up at a thrift store, shopping with your best friend, when you should be teaching school.

Go to bed. I'm a night owl, and I understand how peaceful it can be when everyone is tucked quietly in their beds sleeping. It seems like you can have your own indulgent time and get so much done, but, actually, it's harder for you to be productive when you stay up late at night. One of the most obvious reasons is because the later you stay up, the harder it is to get up early in the morning, and you'll start your day behind schedule.

Now, I understand that different families have different routines, and I know not everyone can go to bed early and get up early. What I recommend in that instance is for you to set a time that you plan to start school and stick with it, and if you made sure to get your house in order before you went to bed the night before, then you should have a much easier and more organized day.

Friends. I'm not saying friends are time-wasters, but I'm saying you need to keep a time for friends and a time *not* for friends. Make sure to set limits and boundaries, and don't be afraid to say no. Your homeschool and teaching your kids has to come before spending time with your friends.

Find and identify *your* time wasters and then do your best to avoid them. The things that tempt me may not tempt you, and vice versa, so you need to do a thorough evaluation of the things that take time away from you accomplishing your main goals.

Get a Good Organizer

In order to be a good keeper of the home, you need to have a way to organize all your responsibilities. Find a system that works for you. I happen to be an analog girl in a digital world. I like pen and paper to write down everything I need to remember. Some people work well with an online or digital system, and that's great; just find something that will help you to keep your home, family, and time organized.

A popular trend right now is the Bullet Journal. A Bullet Journal is a way to organize anything you want to in a fancy and artistic way. You start out with a blank notebook and make it into whatever kind of planner or organizer you like. I've seen some really neat looking Bullet

Journals, but I'm not a very artistic person myself and struggled with the creative side of it. I found that the Bullet Journal actually weighed me down instead of helping me accomplish what it should have, but that might not be the case for you. You may just want to check it out. If you're a techie girl, feel free to use your phone; just find something to help you manage your time.

You Need a Plan to Minimize Appointments

One of the benefits of being a homeschooling mom is that you can fit in appointments at times when others can't. For example, we're able to see our chiropractor during a normal school day, while others aren't and that can be a dubious blessing.

It's easy to blow off your homeschool day, but you want to make sure school is your top priority. Try to organize your appointments on one particular day of the month or week. More kids equals more appointments, so be on the lookout for how you can maximize your schedule by keeping your appointments on one day. That way, if you have to be out of the house, you can pack meals and plan for a day out and get right back into your school schedule the next day. Rather than having one appointment each day of the week, you'll organize your time much better by keeping all your appointments on the same day.

You Need a Plan for Meals

It seems like every time I turn around, someone is hungry. Meals come three times a day *every* day, and if your family is anything like mine, they're also looking for snacks in between. Feeding your family and taking the time to do it well is one of the best ways you can show your family they're a top priority to you, but you definitely need to plan.

There are many good choices. Many people, much smarter than I, have developed plans and systems for you to organize your meal planning. You don't have to look far online to see that there's a meal planning service begging for you to purchase it at every corner. Many meal planning services even offer free trials. You can do cooking once a month, batch cooking, weekly meal planning, menu planning services, you name it; it's out there for you to try.

I've tried many plans and found parts of each I like. There is no perfect plan, just like there is no perfect family. I encourage you to find a plan and use it, and don't be afraid to change it if it's not working. You might consider investing some of your grocery money into a meal planning subscription if it's a service that really makes menu planning easier for you, but make sure you actually use the plan and aren't just paying a monthly fee for something that's sitting in your email inbox untouched.

I've found that lunches are especially difficult for homeschooling moms partly because, if you're like me, the homeschool day goes right up until lunch and then continues as soon as we're done eating. I don't know about you, but I don't have a personal chef to prepare meals for me, so I'm the one responsible for taking care of meals.

I've found a few tricks to help me with lunch. One is a new product called the "Hot Logic." It's a mini oven that fits inside a thermal, insulated holder for a 9" by 13" cake pan. It also comes in a miniature version. You put food in it in the morning and plug it in, and it warms the food and holds it at a temperature that's ready to be served. This has made a ton of difference for me in preparing lunches. I can make extra food the night before, and when cleaning up for supper, put it in the pan so it's ready for morning. Then, after cleaning up from breakfast, I put it in the insulated tote and plug it in. I just have to make sure and remember to actually do that! It's been beneficial for me to know lunch is sitting, warming on the counter, and I can teach until about fifteen minutes before my husband comes home for lunch.

Recently, I saw an article online about a woman who prepares lunches for her kids just like she would if they were going off to school. After supper the night before, she and her kids prepare a few lunches for a couple days out. They get them ready and put them in the refrigerator so they're prepared for the next day. Kids can then grab their meals whenever they're hungry and the word is all done. Our family eats lunch together at the same time each day, so this system wasn't practical for me, but you may find it helpful. I have also found slow-cookers to be a lifesaver. Stick something in the slow cooker in the morning, and it'll be ready for lunch or supper, whichever you choose.

Menu planning will help you be a good steward of your time and money, and since preparing meals is one of the responsibilities of the keeper of the home, you'll feel so much better if you have a plan in place.

The financial implications of a grocery budget are huge, and we'll get into that more in Chapter Eleven. I've found that when I fail to plan, we spend way more money on low-quality food when I go shopping. However, if I plan and am ready with ideas for meals, I can make our money stretch much further. The grocery budget is the one area of the household finances I'm in charge of, and I want to honor God with it. *I've often* prayed and asked God for wisdom to manage that money well. Our family has tons of food allergies; therefore, menu planning is essential for me to make sure I can get something for everyone to eat.

If it's possible, consider making grocery shopping a date time. I've really come to appreciate grocery shopping with my husband as a fun and special time we spend together. We have kids that are old enough to babysit for us, but if you don't, consider hiring a babysitter or swap with a friend. If that's not possible, make grocery shopping a special time with your kids. As the keeper of the home, feeding your family is one of the most special ways you can show your family you love them. By taking the time to prepare tasty and healthy meals for them, *you'll show* them you care. After all, "The way to the heart is through the belly." It just takes thought and preparation and a little bit of time, but I know the efforts are worth it.

Practice Hospitality

Sadly, hospitality is becoming a lost art. As more and more families turn away from the dinner table and get frantically more busy, people are not eating together as often. This means inviting a family over to your house for dinner is going to be even less common, but hospitality is a God-ordained thing (1 Peter 4:9). We talked previously about the importance of showing your kids how to serve and be welcoming by having company into your homes. In doing so, you'll teach them a great example of what service to others looks like.

But don't save your best for your company. Your family also needs to feel your hospitality. Have you ever been cleaning your house and had one of your kids ask, "Who's coming over?" I don't know about you, but I have, and it makes me cringe. I want my family to feel like I give them my best, so as important as it is to have others over, it's also important to show hospitality to your own family. Don't neglect setting a nice table and sharing your best dishes with your kids. They will remember what an awesome thing it was that you took the time and cared. Almost every night dinner is rushed for some reason or another, and it's tempting to throw dishes on the table as quickly as I can without putting much thought into what I'm doing, but every so often it's important to sit back and relax and have a hospitable dinner together with your family.

Sometimes, if I can manage the grocery money well enough, we will treat our kids to a steak dinner. The kids love to help set the table with nice, fancy dishes and pretty tablecloth. They like to set up candles and enjoy a time of quiet talking together around the table.

It's a good time for the kids to practice self-control and participate in the conversation. By showing hospitality to your family, *you'll show* them you enjoy what you do and you see serving them as the keeper of your home is as a privilege and not a burden.

The Game Plan:

- Evaluate your friendships. Ask yourself how your friends influence your view of your responsibilities at home. Are they affecting you for the good or the bad? Decide if you need to change any of your friendships, and, if so, pray about how to do so.
- Identify areas in your life that tempt you to compare your house with something you can't or don't have. Is Pinterest or any other social media a problem? Develop an attitude of gratitude by listing the things in your house you're thankful for. Begin to be intentionally thankful for your house when you have chores you don't enjoy doing.
- Find an area of your life that needs to be organized. If there is more than one, start with the smallest and most easily completed task and move on from there. Develop a plan to start organizing those areas that are most bothersome to you and commit to completing one task per week.
- Make a meal plan. It can be simple or elaborate. Use the internet or your local library to find options. Once you decide on a plan, commit to sticking to it.
- Plan a special family dinner where you serve your loved ones the very best. You might even include the kids in planning the menu and the place settings. Enjoy a quiet and relaxed evening together.

Chapter 8
Balancing the Priority
Of Cultivating
Meaningful Friendships

"Friendship is born at that moment when one person says to another: What! You too? I thought I was the only one."

~ C.S. Lewis

Homeschooling takes a lot of support, and friendships are definitely important; they can make or break you. Not everyone understands homeschooling. In fact, my experience is that most people don't understand homeschooling. Unfortunately, sometimes it's your friends who understand the least, but that's okay. When you homeschool, friendships will definitely change. Some will strengthen, and some will fade. It's okay to realize friendships are all constantly evolving, and they sometimes only last for a season.

Essentially, your husband needs to be your best friend. Now, I understand this isn't the case for everyone and not every husband will understand homeschooling either, even if he is your best friend. Don't be disappointed. Even if he's not into homeschooling or doesn't understand it, or if your relationship isn't rock-solid, still include him in anything you can. Talk to him about homeschooling in general and make sure to talk to him about your homeschooling day. Include him in the purchasing of your curriculum and talk to him about your fears and concerns. You may find that by including him in this way, eventually, he will start to understand homeschooling and maybe even become your best friend, if he's not already.

Iron Sharpens Iron

Rather than looking for a sea of friends, try to find one good friend who will stand by you no matter what. Seek out an "iron sharpens iron" relationship. Proverbs 22:17 (NIV) says, "As iron sharpens iron, so one person sharpens another." Several years ago, I was praying that God would send me a good friend who was more than just someone I could hang out with. I was looking for a deeper friendship, a friend who would encourage me and hold me accountable and for whom I could do the same in return.

God answered my prayers and sent me more than I could have ever asked for. He sent me my very own "iron sharpens iron" friend, and I *couldn't be* more grateful. Together, we have read through the Bible in the course of a year, checking in with each other *every* day. We've prayed for and with each other, cried together, laughed (a ton) together, encouraged each other when we were discouraged, and held each other accountable to be God-honoring wives and homeschooling mothers.

We have an app on each of our phones called Marco Polo, which allows us to video chat in real time. That means, just like a text, I send her a video, and when she has time, she can watch it and respond. This is invaluable. There have been many times during my homeschool day when *I've needed* someone to listen. I can send her a quick message, and, when she's able to, she can respond and encourage me to keep doing what I'm doing or steer me in another direction. She offers encouragement and oftentimes a Bible verse. She has been one of the biggest blessings in my life!

Begin to pray that God will send you a friend who will hold you accountable and lift you up when you need it, but, more importantly, that this friend will steer you in the direction of Christ and not be afraid to tell you if she sees you taking a turn for the worst. You need an "iron sharpens iron" friend for both accountability and encouragement. Homeschooling is definitely not for the faint of heart, and there are days you need someone to listen to you as well as a shoulder to cry on.

It should go without saying, but as a homeschooling *mom*, you need your friend to be a *she*. Never develop an accountability friendship with a man. It's dangerous to your marriage and disrespectful to your husband. I recommend that you not develop any deep friendships with people of the opposite sex.

Your friend also needs to 'get' homeschooling. Ideally, she should be a homeschooler herself. She should understand that the homeschool day is tedious and takes a lot of time and effort. If you could find a veteran or retired homeschooler, it would be even be better. Whoever you find to be your accountability partner needs to be somebody you feel comfortable with. You need to be able to tell her what's on your heart.

Make a system to check in with each other on a regular basis and talk about how homeschooling is going. Tell her not to let you off the hook. After all, that's the point of accountability!

Also, evaluate your friendship with her by asking yourself:

• Does she draw you closer to Christ?
• Does she encourage you to draw closer to your husband?
• Does she encourage you to draw closer to your family?
• Does she keep you on track with homeschooling?

Make sure to pray for and with each other. Prayer requests come up naturally during everyday conversation, but if you would like to be more pointed about it, you can always ask specifically what requests your friend has. When you're homeschooling, you don't have a lot of extra time, so be careful to help encourage each other to make your homes and your families the top priority.

Be Careful

A word of caution: While finding a good friend is a blessing, be careful with "girls' night out" or repetitive time away from your family. It's fun and entertaining, but it can become addictive. Be wise with your time and careful not to crave "girls' night out", seeing it as an escape from your family. Don't hear me say it's not okay to spend time with your friend, but, ultimately, she should be encouraging you toward your family, not away.

Also, be careful not to dump on your friend. You don't want to take advantage of her kindness by continually complaining to her about how bad your homeschool day is going. Of course, there are times you'll need her to help you get out from feeling down in the dumps, but instead of complaining to her, try more of a troubleshooting approach. Share your problems with her, but then listen intently for her advice and be willing to implement it and be willing to return the favor. She will likely need a listening ear and a shoulder to cry on at some point, too. Make sure you're willing to be as good a friend as you're asking her to be. Make sure you're giving as much as you're receiving.

Realize Your Friend is a Treasure

As I mentioned earlier, your friendships definitely change when you homeschool, so finding one good friend is a treasure you must hang on to. You might find your other friends have all left you by the wayside while you do this crazy thing called homeschooling. Just realize that's totally okay, and you'll make it through.

What if You're Having Trouble Finding a Friend?

If you're having trouble finding a friend who will encourage you, pray and ask God to send you someone. Church is a great place to look for a friend. You'd be surprised how many ladies are also lonely. I've also found joy in friendships with older women who wouldn't seem like a likely friend for me. If you take the time to get to know someone you never thought of as a friend, you might be surprised at how a relationship can develop.

Your local homeschool co-op is another great place to look. There, you'll probably find like-minded people, since they're also homeschooling. Don't be afraid to invite someone over and practice hospitality. Get out of your comfort zone and reach out to somebody you might not otherwise talk to. You never know. It might just be the start of something big!

If God isn't allowing a friend in your life right now, you may find that you have a hidden gem right before your eyes. Your kids can actually become really good friends. Sometimes, you just need to invest in them instead of friendships. As a result, you'll be come a very close-knit family. You'll be able to develop a strong family unit.

What to do When Your Non-homeschooling Friends Don't Understand

Generally speaking, people are intrigued by homeschooling, but, for the most part, they just don't understand. I have actually had people ask me why I'd keep my kids home all day long instead of sending them off to school. Your non-homeschooling friends may not understand why you do what you do. Don't feel like you have to talk about homeschooling with them. In most instances, they're concerned that you might try to convert them to your way of thinking.

I've found that letting them initiate conversations about school is the best way to handle their skepticism. Wait for them to ask questions and don't talk about homeschooling unless they want to know. Most importantly, never come across as judgmental to your friends who don't homeschool. More than likely, they feel uncomfortable around you because they feel like you might be judging them.

That's why it's important to find like-minded homeschooling families you and your family can become friends with. If you're blessed enough to find a homeschooling family, then hopefully you'll get along with the adults, and your kids will become friends with their kids. It can be a strong and solid, lasting relationship.

Having Only Kids Around Can be Difficult

At the end of the school day, sometimes, I feel like all I've done is correct papers, teach phonics, and explain how to memorize times tables. I crave time with my friends, and it's easy for loneliness to set in. That doesn't mean I don't enjoy homeschooling or prefer not to be with my kids. It just means that after a long, hard day of teaching, I enjoy adult conversation. A quick conversation with my "iron sharpens iron" friend helps revive my spirit. Proverbs 17:22 (NIV) says, "A cheerful heart is good medicine, but a crushed spirit dries up the bones." It's important for us to have friends we can turn to.

Don't My Kids Need Friends, Too?

Whenever anyone finds out that I homeschool, it seems like they always ask the same questions: What do you do for science? Do you have a microscope? And…How do your kids get socialized? As I talked about in Chapter Six, the main relationship I'm concerned about is between my kids and their siblings. We work hard to have strong sibling friendships so they can grow up to really love each other.

The first answer I give people who ask that question is that we have built-in friendships. Family friendships are important, but, certainly, I know what they're getting at. Our kids do need to be socialized, and they do need friendships. I've also found that the older my kids get, the more important relationships are for them. I spend time praying for our kids' friends. I pray that they would develop godly friendships with other like-minded kids.

Church is an important way for your kids to meet friends. I do as much as I can to encourage relationships between my kids and the kids at church. Whenever possible, I encourage my kids to get together with their friends from church. Sometimes, that may come as a sacrifice. It's not always easy to orchestrate schedules and make sure my kids have time to spend with other like-minded kids, but I'm willing to make sacrifices to ensure my kids can get together with their church friends, even if it means a little inconvenience for me.

Friendships Will Look Different

It's also important to think about friendships on a different level than the normal traditional view. Typically speaking, most kids in public school will have three or four good friends in their class. They'll all be the same age and will likely have the same interests. They'll play ball together at recess or spend time doing the same activities during class, but when you homeschool, your kids will have the opportunity to make relationships on different levels.

My kids have a very good friend they all love to spend time with. They fish together, eat donuts together, and spend time playing cribbage. Now, you might think this friend is a little boy the same age as my kids, but he's actually a bachelor in his sixties, not a very likely friend for a nine-year-old, but because we've encouraged our kids to have friendships on different levels, they can relate to people who aren't necessarily their own age. To me, this is one of the joys and benefits of homeschooling, so don't be afraid to branch out and let your kids make friendships on other levels. As homeschoolers, your kids' friendships may not look as traditional as you might expect.

The Game Plan:

- Evaluate your friendships using the following questions:
  - Does she draw you closer to Christ?
  - Does she encourage you to draw closer to your husband?
  - Does she encourage you to draw closer to your family?
  - Does she keep you on track with homeschooling?
- Work hard at being a good friend. Make sure you're attentive and available within the confines of your homeschool schedule. Take time to spend with your friend.
- Find an accountability partner if you don't already have one. Check in with each other on a regular basis and make sure you share your struggles as well as your victories, but also be willing to *be* a good friend and accountability partner. Try hard not to become self-centered.
- Develop friendships with each of your kids by getting to know their likes and dislikes. Spend time doing something fun together on a regular basis.

Chapter 9
Balancing the Priority Of Finding time for Fun

"A merry heart does good like medicine."
~ Proverbs 17:22 (NKJV)

While having fun doesn't seem like it should be a top priority; sometimes, you just need to let go and be crazy! As a homeschooling mom, you need to take time out for fun. School can bring so much tension that, sometimes, you just need to step back and relax. There's a temptation to become way too focused on academics; it's important to take time off.

If you're like me, it might be hard to shut off the teacher in you. I find myself correcting grammar at the dinner table or teaching my kids times tables in the store. I know there isn't anything actually wrong with that, but sometimes you need to just be a mom. It's easy to become too serious and focused on homeschooling. Trust me when I tell you that you don't want your kids to think you *never* have fun. Nor do your kids need to know how stressed you are.

They need to see you kick back and have a good time. They also need to have playful and fun interaction with you. I remember doing many fun things with my mom growing up. When I was in high school, it was all the rage to cruise up and down Main Street. On a Friday night, most of the local kids who were popular could be found circling the town in a cool car. Our town was built in a figure-eight shape. Kids would cruise down Main Street, into the local park, and back up Main Street into the McDonald's parking lot, where they would turn around and do it again.

I don't know what the craze was, but kids talked about it all day long on Fridays at school. Are you going cruising tonight? Who are you going with? Maybe I'll catch up with you. Maybe I'll see you...Do you know what I did? I cruised up and down Main Street. Oh yes! Until all hours of the night. I'd even get ice cream at McDonalds and talk to my friends at stop lights. We would laugh and joke and have fun as we ran into each other on the crazy loop all around town.

But do you know who I did it with? My mom! And do you know who sat in the back seat of our car? Some of the coolest kids in high school! Why? Because my mom was fun, and everybody wanted to be with us. We had so many fits of laughter and huge memories cruising up and down Main Street! Actually, one time, we even had the idea to toilet paper a friend's house. Now, I'm not saying I condone it, but from a kid's perspective, it was pretty fun!

My parents were always having fun with my sister and me. My dad took time to fly kites with us and go out for special breakfast dates. We spent time going to the park, riding bikes, ice skating, etc. I'm sure my dad still has a bad hip from the time I tripped him, and we both fell on the ice! Instead of hollering in pain, we laid on the ice and talked about what characters we saw in the clouds. I later found out my dad was in too much pain to get up!

We did random, fun things together as a family. I look back with fondness on the family memories my parents created for me, and I know fun was a very important part of my growing up. Don't get me wrong; I was taught responsibility and the value of hard work, but we celebrated small achievements and had fun at any opportunity.

I want my kids to say the same thing about me. I want them to remember a mom who felt like having fun was just as important as knowing how to conjugate verbs and do long division. The thing about having fun together is that kids just want you to take the time. They don't care if you make a huge fancy plan and spend lots of money. You don't have to take a cross-country vacation in order to have fun with your kids. You just need to spend time doing the little things.

At our house, we usually have a running game of Rook or Memory set up on the dining room table. Throughout the day, we take time to play games with our kids. I'll be the first to admit I'm not much of a game player; I'm much more into reading books to the kids or doing a craft, but I know the kids feel special and important when I take time to play a game with them. When you take time to have fun with your kids, you'll see a change in their behavior. They will want to please you more. Your kids will open their hearts to you.

It Starts By Having Fun with Your Kids

Do you know what's neat about having fun with your kids? Eventually, it makes them want to be with you. Just like me with my mom, cruising down Main Street on a Friday night, your kids will want to spend time with you because they'll know you care.

Spending time together and having fun gives you a great foundation for relationships. Eventually, and trust me when I say this, there will be a time when you need to talk to your kids. It might be about the dangers of premarital sex or questions about truthfulness, but if you've taken the time to build a foundation for your relationship, then your kids will be much more likely to open up to you and let you have their heart.

It seems like a small thing, but when you give your kids your time and play with them, they'll behave much better. Try to take the time to play first before doing other things. I've found that if I spend half an hour playing with my kids, which isn't a lot of time, they're more likely to spend time playing by themselves.

Someday, They Won't Ask

This kills me. I understand what it's like to be deep into a project and have your little one come and ask if you'll play cars with him, but they won't be asking you to have fun with them forever. There will be a day when the last little car is picked up, and the dolls are all put away. No one will be asking if you can play with him.

Don't wait for the right time. You'll never be done with everything. I can promise you there will always be projects and things waiting for your attention, but your kids won't always be in your home, and time really does fly by quickly. Try taking just half an hour to play, and you'll be amazed at what a difference it makes in your kids' lives.

You've heard me say that the family that prays together stays together. Well, the same is true of play. A close-knit family is often characterized by their ability to laugh and have fun together. You can build a foundation for long-lasting relationships right now, simply by spending time having fun with your kids.

How do You Want your Kids to Remember You?

Being fun and silly doesn't come naturally to me. When I finally let loose, I really enjoy it, but I'm very task-oriented and I like to get things done. My idea of fun is cleaning out the garage or getting a project done. I know! I'm boring, but I don't want my kids to think I'm always serious. I don't want them to look back and think I never knew how to have fun with them. Look at the memories I have of my parents and how fun they were (and still are)! I want my kids to be able to say they had fun with me, too!

When I look back, I realize my mom was my best friend. And do you know what? We still have a great relationship today. She must have known what she was doing because it made for a great relationship with her grandkids as well, so there's another added benefit.

Be Silly

I already mentioned cruising up and down Main Street with my mom and the fun things my dad and I did together, but as I sat down to think about the memories, many things came to mind. One night, when my mom was folding clothes, and my sister and I were sitting talking to her, she tossed a pair of socks across the living room for me to put away. The socks got caught in the ceiling fan and went flying across the room. The three of us looked at each other with a shocked expression, and then my mom shrugged her shoulders and threw another pair of socks. Just like the first time, the socks went flying through the air as they hit the fan, and we all started to laugh.

You can imagine what happened next. I picked up the socks my mom threw at me and threw them back at her, only they ended up in the kitchen as the fan catapulted them through the air, so my mom picked up a shirt and threw it into the fan, and it whipped around and went flying. Then, my sister picked up some more laundry and threw it into the fan. Suddenly, all three of us were throwing laundry into the fan and laughing hysterically until tears ran down our cheeks. We must have done that for half an hour. I know; we're easily entertained!

We laughed gut-wrenching laughs and couldn't control the tears streaming down our faces. As we were finally starting to die down, my dad walked in the door, clothed in his painting uniform after a hard day of work. We sobered up. Confused, my dad slowly looked around at the trail of clean laundry strewn across the living room floor. Socks, shirts, and other unmentionables hung from picture frames, the corner of the TV, the lamp, and every other object in the room. The look on his face was enough to send us into hysterics. All he could ask was, "Wh-at happened?" We laughed so hard; we couldn't even explain it to him. We still laugh about it years later.

The best part? It was silly, provided entertainment, and didn't cost a dime. It wasn't planned; it just happened because our home was a place where we knew how to have good old-fashioned fun, and from a child's perspective, it was fun to see my mom let loose and to have fun with her.

Interestingly enough, as I'm writing this chapter, my kids are spending the night at my parents' house. One of my sons just called me and said, "Grandma is so much fun, and it sounds like you had a really fun childhood as you were growing up!" I'm not exactly sure what they were talking about, but I'm glad the fun is carrying on to the next generation!

Take Time to Have Fun on a Daily, Weekly, and Yearly Basis

Obviously, you can't make every day a carnival ride, but you should take some time out to enjoy your kids, even if it's just a moment. My little kids love it when I read a book to them, and the big kids enjoy playing a game around the dining room table. As I said before, I'm very task-oriented, and it's hard for me to stop what I'm doing and play, but it's definitely necessary for my kids' well-being. Do you know what? It's good for me, too! I know it will cement our relationship and build a great foundation.

Weekly traditions are fun, too. You might consider having a weekly custom such as "Taco Tuesday" and play games afterwards, or you can plan a movie night where you pop popcorn and make fun snacks. Keep it simple so you're more likely to do it. If you make it too involved, you won't want to execute it, and it will be easier to let it go.

Our family enjoys friendly competition. The kids love playing various basketball games together with Dad on the driveway court. We like things like cup-stacking competitions and made-up ball games. We also love playing family bowling on the Wii. Our six-year-old daughter loves playing Memory. One year for her birthday, we took the entire day and rotated shifts of playing Memory with her. She had so much fun and felt like a princess because everyone was playing *her* game!

You can do just about anything with your kids and make it fun. Coloring, puzzles, organized games...you can set up a battalion of army guys to launch attacks on a building block fort. My kids have always loved playing army guys or race cars in a cake pan of uncooked oatmeal. It makes an excellent "sand box" on a cold winter day. You could also build a fort. Kids love building forts. Be creative!

There are, of course, the things that come around on a yearly rotation such as Christmas, Thanksgiving, birthdays, etc., but what about making your own traditions? About eight years ago, our family started doing the Fox Family Olympics. (I went into detail and covered the specifics about the Fox Family Olympics in Chapter Six.) In addition to the Fox Family Olympics, we have developed some fun traditions that have lasted over the years, even though you already know I'm not great with keeping traditions. Here are some of the fun ideas we have done:

On Valentine's Day, we do Dollar Store shopping. We let each of our kids draw a name from a hat and then give them each three or four dollars. Then, we go to the local Dollar Store, and the kids sneak around behind each other's backs while they buy something they think the person whose name they drew would like. My heart swells, and I smile as I see my kids carefully choosing something they think their sibling would like. Then, we come home and have some Valentine's Day snacks and give each other our gifts. It's neat to see what the kids pick out for each other, and I chuckle to myself as I think about my sixteen-year-old son buying hair bows for his little sister.

One year, I overheard the cashier tell my seven-year-old son that he couldn't buy a lighter without an ID. He looked at her confused and said, "But I'm buying it for my daddy!" Naturally, I stepped in to help him buy the lighter and then explained to her that several more kids would be coming through on their own to pay for their purchases. She asked what we were doing, and I told her. She thought it was very neat!

We also do a similar tradition on Christmas Eve with our stockings. Just put some time into thinking about ways you can have fun together as a family and then make it happen. Like I said before, it doesn't have to be intricate or expensive or even time-consuming. Just have fun together.

Take Time to Unplug

Hopefully, I've convinced you by now that it's important to spend time together as a family and have fun doing it. Let me encourage you to unplug from your devices while spending time together. Too many families are not communicating with each other and instead are living in a virtual world. Please unplug your electronics for a set amount of time and just talk to your kids. Make it a time you're totally committed to spending time with your kids, and they're with you. Be present and in the moment. This is hard to do if everyone has an electronic device.

Spend Time Individually With Your Kids

If you have more than one child, it's especially important to schedule time with your kids individually. I mentioned earlier that my dad took me out for breakfast when I was a kid. It was our tradition to do breakfast together, and I felt like I could talk to him about anything. I really enjoyed the time I got with just my dad and no other distractions. Our tradition carried on right up until the day I got married and is now being executed with my kids. In fact, when we were last at my parents' house, my daughter said, "Mom please wake me up if Grandpa decides to go out for breakfast!"

Ben and I make it a point to do the same thing with our kids. Sometimes, my husband and I both take one of our kids out for a meal so we can share special, uninterrupted time together with just that child, and, sometimes, they go with just one of us. We want our kids to feel like they have access to us even though we have several kids.

Another fun thing to do is a kid date night. Kids especially love this because they get to stay up while everyone else has to go to bed. I love fondue. It's one of my favorite date night activities. When I had the idea to share it with one of our kids, it went over well! If you have never done fondue, you have to try it! You deep fry various things at the table while you sit and visit. It's a great way to linger over your food and talk to your kids one at a time. Our kids feel like this is a special privilege, and we enjoy taking the individual time with them.

Are You Lacking Ideas?

Be creative and don't put too much pressure on yourself. It's more about spending time together than what you do. As I said earlier, kids are happy just spending time with you. Just remember to be silly and let loose. If you're stuck, here are some ideas:

Build a fort together. Kids absolutely love making forts. The more rooms, the better! If you're feeling adventurous, you could even let them sleep in it. Whenever my kids make a fort, I always make a special snack and let them take it into the fort.

Pop some popcorn and read a book together. This is especially fun when the weather is cold. Curl up with a blanket and snuggle up for a fun story.

Listen to an audio drama together as a family. Our family has really enjoyed Jonathan Park, The Brinkman Adventures, and Adventures in Odyssey. We love listening to the adventures of each of these stories, as well as the neat Biblical truths they teach.

Watch a movie together. This isn't one of my top favorites because it doesn't involve as much communication, but sometimes it's just fun to snuggle in together and watch a movie. Netflix has some good kid's movies if you don't have a good library of your own. Don't forget the popcorn and snacks!

Late night date nights. I haven't met a kid yet who doesn't like this idea. Tuck your kids into bed like normal. Don't let them know anything out of the ordinary is about to happen. Wait about ten minutes and then get them up and take them for a special treat or a ride around the park. Again, it doesn't have to be expensive. It's the thought that counts!

Cook or bake something together. Kids love to be in the kitchen, and it's a great family activity to do together. As an added bonus, you'll have a nice treat when you're finished. There are many ideas online for cute kid's food and family treats. You can even have a contest to see who can create the craziest thing out of certain ingredients.

Tell stories. Kids love to hear stories about your childhood. They want to know what it was like when you were a kid and what things you enjoy doing. My kids always want us to share embarrassing moments. They think it's funny to hear about the times we were goofy, and it's a great way to pass on your family's history.

Look through family photo albums. It's fun for kids to reminisce about their younger days and see their own siblings when they were younger. There can be a lot of laughs, and it also helps your kids remember family members who have passed away or who might live far away.

"Minute to Win It" games. We have enjoyed setting up "Minute to Win It" games to play together as a family. This is when you have a task to complete in less than a minute, such as stacking cups. They always create a lot of laughs.

Learn jokes. One of our kids is a huge jokester. He has loved a good joke since he was old enough to tell his first "knock-knock" joke. I'm always trying to find new jokes to tell him because he appreciates them so much.

Laugh! Laugh a lot! Laugh at your mistakes. Laugh at anything that's funny. Laugh at jokes. Just laugh. Laughing together creates memories and helps ease the stress of everyday life.

Pinterest. You can always look at Pinterest for just about anything you need. Pinterest will point you in the right direction for fun family times.

Remember it's about spending time together as a family and having fun while doing it. It doesn't have to be elaborate or expensive. Having fun together grows family relationships. You have a unique opportunity as a homeschooling family to spend fun time together because you're together much more than the family whose kids are in school all day. Enjoy your time!

Hobbies are Another Part of Having Fun

Homeschooling moms are people, too, and as such, they need to spend time enjoying things for themselves. Obviously, this comes with a balance, but I want to encourage you that, as a homeschooling mom, you still need to have hobbies. It's okay to take time away from the kids and spend it doing something you really enjoy. More than likely, before you started homeschooling, you had things you did with your time other than grading spelling papers and reading history books. Don't feel bad spending some time to do things that you enjoy, but don't become overindulgent.

You can be free of feeling guilty, like you're neglecting the rest of your family if you take time to do something that you enjoy. Spending time on your hobbies will actually rejuvenate you and make you a better teacher, wife, and mother. In fact, doing something you enjoy is a good way to reduce stress. As a homeschooling mom, you have already given up so much. Maybe it was the dream of a career, or maybe you even had a job you left to homeschool. Whatever the case, your time is selflessly given to your kids, teaching them faithfully each day. Homeschooling is a sacrifice that comes at a cost, most of which is your time. Therefore, a hobby is a good reward for all your hard work.

You might find it necessary to schedule time for yourself. I'm blessed with a husband who sees the importance of my spending time doing a hobby, but if that's not feasible in your house, for whatever reason, you may need to schedule child care or swap with a friend. Most stay-at-home moms are willing to share child care, since they know the value of having some time away from their kids in order to refresh.

You could consider doing your hobby when your kids are in bed. I've finished many sewing projects at 3:00 in the morning just because I appreciate the uninterrupted time. Granted, my eyes were going cross-eyed, and I've nearly sewn my fingers together, but there isn't anything like not having to stop to help someone in the bathroom or fix a snack! Just don't make it a habit to stay up too late every night!

Keep the Right Attitude

Please be careful with time. There's a danger in getting addicted to having your own time. I've found that it's a little like sugar. The more you have, the more you want, and more doesn't always satisfy. You'll always want more. In that case, be grateful for the time you *do* get to spend doing your hobbies and remember you can always come back to them. There will always be another time to do it again.

Also, keep limited expectations. With kids in the house, you never know what might come up and interrupt the time you had scheduled, and that's totally okay. If you keep your expectations low, you won't be disappointed. Consider the ditch digger. A ditch digger doesn't get discouraged because he knows the only thing he has to do is to dig a ditch. He's not looking for greener grass on the other side of the fence or a better scenario. He embraces the fact that what he's doing is digging a ditch; therefore, nothing makes him feel discouraged.

With that in mind, try to think with low expectations and don't be upset when things don't go exactly as planned, and, finally, when your kids interrupt you, remember that "Children are not a distraction from more important work. They're the most important work." This quote is often attributed to C.S. Lewis, but no one really knows who first said this. Whoever it was knew what they were talking about!

No Guilt! Just Enjoy!

Now, sometimes, it's okay to include your kids in your hobbies, and there are certainly times when it's fun to do things with your kids, like teaching them how to bake or do a craft, but in this instance, we're talking about spending time doing your own hobbies, and you don't have to feel guilty about doing that. Sometimes, you need to spend time alone. I for one, enjoy a quiet room where I can think all by myself. Undoubtedly, I can't do that all day long, or even on a daily basis, but I do know that when I spend time alone, working on something I enjoy, I feel refreshed and ready to serve my family again.

Include your Husband

If you choose not to spend your time alone, I'd suggest inviting your husband along. Maybe the two of you used to have interests together that have changed since having kids and starting homeschooling. Have your common interests left?

Work hard to find something the two of you can do together. It's important that you preserve your marriage now because your kids won't always be with you. There will be a time when it's just the two of you, and if you make it a priority to do things together now, you'll have an easier time transitioning into an empty nest when the time comes, and it will. I've been told it comes sooner than you think and sooner than you're ready, so work now to develop hobbies with your husband. When the time comes, you'll be happy you did.

Be Careful not to Overspend

Hobbies can get very expensive. It's okay to spend money on yourself, provided your budget and husband allow for it, but keep your eyes open as you realize hobbies are not cheap. I've been guilty of purchasing products and supplies for hobbies and never doing them. It's easy to overspend.

On the other hand, I have also made many things that have been useful for our family as a result of having a hobby. One such instance was a calendar I made for my 'iron sharpens iron" friend. I make vinyl signs. It was her birthday, and I was in the mood to make a craft, so I decided to make her a Family Celebrations Calendar. You may have seen them online before. This calendar is a board with the word "family" on it along with all the months of the year. Disks hang from each month to indicate family members' birthdays.

I was so excited to give it to her, and she loved it! But then I had an idea. What if I tried to sell my hobby? This was something I really enjoyed doing, so I thought, "Why not make another calendar and actually earn money doing it?" I did what anybody would do. I posted it on Facebook without any real knowledge of selling anything and not really even knowing how to get supplies to make them. My husband helped me make my friend's calendar, and it was rigged up in such a way we couldn't reproduce it.

Being my naive self, I didn't just post it to *one* Facebook group but several. Within an hour, I had *six* orders for *six* calendars! I was so excited and terrified at the same time I had never sold anything for profit, and, like I said before, I had no idea where to even get the supplies! But that's true to my character. I often act before I think things through all the way. Thankfully, I have a level-headed husband who helped me sort out the mess. He simply said, "Let's get to work!" and that started a four-year business of sign-making at Christmas time!

You might consider turning your hobby into a small business to help earn an income for your family, but don't put too much pressure on yourself. After all, the idea is to refresh yourself and rejuvenate. It'll take away the fun and defeat the purpose if it gets too out of hand. Trust me! Sign making is no longer my hobby, it's my job! Now, I need to find a new hobby to refresh myself after I'm done working at my old hobby.

Many hobbies can be constructive. If you like to sew, you can make quilts and give them away as gifts. If you like to paint, you can make signs for people. Use your creativity and think of something you can do with your hobbies. You might even consider learning a new hobby. Challenge yourself to do something greater than what you already know how to do.

Sometimes, Reading About Your Hobbies Will Have to be Enough

As parents, we know it's not likely to have unlimited hours of free time to spend on your hobbies. My husband has found a wonderful alternative. He enjoys watching documentaries on YouTube about the hobbies he would *like* to be doing. One time, I asked him why he does that. He said it was because he can't get out to do the hobbies he enjoys, since we're still in the phase of raising our kids, so he's content to watch other people do them. He also likes to read about his hobbies and study how others are executing the hobbies he enjoys. At least, it's good preparation for the day he's able to actually do his hobbies.

Someday, the Kids will be Gone

You'll likely have more time than you know what to do with one day. Different seasons of your life will look different at different times. There will be a day when you have more time than you want. I've listened to a lot of older people say the time goes fast, and the house will be quiet someday. You won't always have a house full of kids, so treasure those precious kids of yours and do something fun together!

The Game Plan:

- What things do you do together as a family that make you laugh and have fun? Evaluate whether you need to add in some fun times and not work so hard. Plan a special game night with your kids and kick back and relax. Enjoy your time and put other responsibilities out of your mind for just a little while.
- Consider a weekly tradition to make memories with your kids. Brainstorm together as a family to come up with ideas you all like. Sundaes on Sunday? Taco Tuesday? Get creative!
- Make a list of the activities each of your children enjoys. Rotate through each activity until you have done something everyone likes. When you're finished, start over with a new list.
- Make a specific time everyone unplugs from all electronics. Determine a preset time and be sure to abide by it. Make it a recurring time, such as every Monday evening or for an hour on Saturdays. Find out what works for your family and then do it.
- Consider your hobbies. Which ones are good to keep pursuing and which need to be set aside until the kids are older? Schedule a time for yourself you can spend doing something fun for yourself.

Chapter 10
Balancing the Priority
Of Teaching your Kids
At Home

"The best learning I had came from teaching."
~ Corrie Ten Boom

This wouldn't be a book for homeschooling moms without a chapter dedicated entirely to homeschooling. After all, as a homeschooling mom, teaching your kids all day long has to be one of your top priorities. I know we've talked about homeschooling all throughout the book, but I wanted to dedicate an entire chapter specifically to the subject of homeschooling itself.

Way back almost 12 years ago, I was completely opposed to homeschooling. In fact, I was actually quoted as saying I'd *never* homeschool my kids. It was partially fear and another part selfishness that kept me from desiring to teach my kids. I couldn't imagine myself as the sole person in charge of another person's academic career. After all, I was a C average student, myself. There are probably some of my former teachers out there who would be completely shocked if they knew I was homeschooling my kids.

Let Go of Your Fears

Whether you decided to homeschool at the very beginning of your motherhood or came into it later, homeschooling in general brings up many fears:

- Am I adequate?
- Am I ruining my kids?
- Am I teaching them enough?
- What if I can't do it?
- What do I do with my little kids?
- Can I afford it?

…and the list goes on. While I wish I could give you a solid answer for every question you have, I really can't, but I can tell you this: You'll *never* be adequate, and you'll *never* be able to teach your kids enough.

You'll have days of success and days of failure. There will be days you wonder why you ever decided to homeschool in the first place. There may even be days you threaten to put your kids in school, but guess what: God is bigger than all your fears and inadequacies, and just like the parable Jesus told of the Widow's Mite (Luke 21:1-4), He can take your tiniest offering you can give and multiply it. Sure, you might not have a college degree or speak Latin, but if you love God and love your kids, God can use the sacrifice you make to homeschool them and multiply your efforts. Let go of your fears.

Why is Homeschooling so Awesome, Anyway?

Like I said before, homeschooling was last on my list of things I'd ever try, but growing up, I had friends who were homeschooled, way before homeschooling was even heard of. There was always some sort of an intrigue in my mind, wondering what it actually was.

As a kid, I thought it would be so cool to learn in your own home. How awesome it must be to have the security of your mom with you, teaching you all day long, and I truly think that, although I was opposed to homeschooling at the beginning of parenting, the thought was there, deep in my roots.

What really makes homeschooling so neat? First of all, *you* get to control what you do with your kids all day, and that's pretty awesome! You're there to handle the teaching and make sure your child is learning what you want him to. If you want your homeschool to be directed more towards literature and arts, you can certainly do that, and if you're more interested in a strong historical core, that's your choice. I personally find it rather fun to tailor my homeschool according to my likes and dislikes, as well as my kids' interests and needs.

We have all heard it said that kids grow up fast, and it really is true, but having my kids home all day allows me to take advantage of the special moments together that I'd otherwise miss if they were in school. In a sense, I feel like homeschooling multiplies the time. Kids still grow up fast, but I get to be a part of what they're doing and spend extra time with them each day.

Homeschooling Helps Sanctify Everyone

Sanctification is simply the process of becoming more like Christ. We become like Him through trials and adversity and by taking advantage of opportunities to grow in godly character. Therefore, in order to grow, we need a certain amount of obstacles. God, in His grace, freely provides opportunities all day long for you and your kids to grow in your sanctification!

I find that my homeschool classroom is one of the greatest places for me to learn how to exercise patience, kindness, gentleness, self-control, and the other fruits of the Spirit. Why? Because I'm with my kids *all day long*, and let me just say, there are teachable moments for all of us each and every day. Kids have opportunities to grow in their sanctification as well. Let's face it, being around your siblings all day long is bound to stir up unpleasant attitudes. For the most part, my kids get along well, but there are definitely moments that arise that are great opportunities to teach Christ-likeness.

Your kids will know you're working on your sanctification by the way you respond when the opportunities to display love come up. Do you exercise patience and self-control when you're frustrated with your kids? Have you ever felt like exploding when you have explained the same math problem over and over again, only to have your child *not* understand *again*? How do you respond when everyone is in need of your attention at the *exact* same time?

Don't worry! No one responds correctly all the time. We all need work, and that's why homeschooling helps to sanctify us. I'll bet that when you were choosing your curriculum, you weren't thinking about how much you would grow into the image of Christ just by teaching your kids each day!

What Happens When Bad Days Come?

Bad attitudes will come. There isn't really any way around it, but bad attitudes don't have to define you. There are days I don't display an attitude of joy when teaching my kids, and the kids know it, so, to begin with, in order to teach my kids to have a good attitude about school, I must first have a good attitude myself.

I don't know what it is about homeschooling, but sometimes it gets the best of me. Perhaps it's the constant neediness or pressure to help everyone at the same time, but there are days I find myself feeling upset and uptight. If this happens to you as well, here are some simple solutions to help you work through your unpleasant feelings.

You must learn to control your anger. I wish I could say I have always done this well, but, unfortunately, that's not the case. I've caught myself speaking in discouraging ways to my kids. That accomplishes nothing more than closing up their hearts, but it's as if something in me won't be satisfied until I let them know how frustrated I'm. My friend, don't make the same mistake I have. You must learn to control your anger.

If anger is a problem for you, I encourage you to find Scripture and commit your heart to the Lord. The Bible talks about how to control our tongues and also what a fierce weapon it can be if we let it get out of control. In my heart, I don't want to be guilty of losing control and being angry, but I fail more often than I'd like to admit. It's okay to use your deficits to teach your kids. They need to see that you're real as well and that you also need Christ and His redeeming work on the cross.

You also need a plan for when you feel the anger rising. It's completely fine to take a minute...or five. Sometimes, I have to tell the kids, "I just need a minute." I take five minutes and step away into a quiet place where I can recite some Scripture to myself, pray, and take a deep breath. When you exercise self-control and walk away for a time until you can come back refreshed and under control, you'll teach your kids that it's possible to deal with anger in a Biblical way.

I like to be proactive. To me, it makes more sense to solve a problem before it even starts. That's why I've found that establishing a healthy Quiet Time routine is probably the *most* effective way to control my anger. You need time to be filled with God's Word, or you'll be teaching from a dry well. What happens if you never feast on the Word of God? From my own experience, your attitude will be the telltale sign, so if you feel like you have been struggling with anger lately, evaluate and ask yourself if you have been spending time with the Lord. (If you find you need extra help, feel free to refer back to Chapter One for help with developing a healthy Quiet Time.)

When the times come that you do fail, and they will, remember to give yourself grace. Nobody does everything perfectly all the time, and being a homeschooling mom is definitely not an easy task. If you have failed, don't beat yourself up. Stop and ask God for forgiveness, and then go to your kids and ask them for forgiveness as well. You would be surprised at how gracious kids can be. Kids are resilient. In fact, there've been times I've really felt like I've blown it. As my kids have gotten older, I have asked them about some of my past failures and the impact they've had on their lives. Their answers were varied, but mostly, I heard that my kids don't really remember my failures. That right there is the grace of God!

However, the times they did remember, they recalled seeing me recognize my need for forgiveness. While I'd never take advantage of this, it sure makes me feel better to know that even though I haven't done everything right, my kids are still okay, so don't be afraid to give yourself grace during the rough times.

What to do When You Don't Feel Like Homeschooling

If the truth be told, there are many days I simply don't feel like doing school, but that's my little secret! Of course, there are times that I'd rather be doing my own thing and not tied to the task of teaching, but if I followed my actions down every path they led, I'd be in big trouble, so on the days you don't feel like homeschooling either, try to override your feelings and do the right thing. Remember? Right actions produce right feelings!

Some days will be a struggle. In fact, I struggle most in the early fall, when the days are still nice, and in the late spring, when the days are beginning to get beautiful outside. I'd much rather be spending time enjoying the weather. Long walks, trips to the park, fun...you name it; I'd rather be doing anything else but teaching at that point, but there's something extra special that comes with knowing you put your all into doing something you didn't feel like doing, and when you're finished with a long, hard homeschool day, it'll feel much better than if you decided not to do anything at all.

There are many reasons why homeschooling gets off track. Unexpected sickness, unforeseen disasters, company...if you took off of school every time something challenging happened, you would never get anything done, so I recommend you have a plan in place that will help you pick up when things start to spiral out of control. If you organize your homeschool classroom and your kids' school work, it'll be much easier to keep working when these things come up, but in the case that you just feel completely overwhelmed, start fresh the next day, even if it's a Friday. Don't wait for Monday; the quicker you get back on track, the better everyone will feel.

How to Do it All

Remember earlier when I let you in on my little secret? Recognizing that you can't do it all, really is a *life-changing* concept. You just can't! You're *one person*, and there's absolutely *no* way for you to do it all. Now you can breathe a sigh of relief, and we can continue to discuss the issue at hand.

I used to pressure myself, thinking I needed to make sure my kids knew everything, and as you just heard me say, there's absolutely no way to do it all, and you'll ever be able to teach your kid everything either. I found a simple solution to overcome this problem. I learned how to teach my kids to be lifetime learners, and there's a simple and fun way to do that. As a family, we started to tackle projects and tasks we knew nothing about. One such instance was a clay pizza oven. If I'd have listened to my own advice and stayed off Pinterest, it may have never happened, but in this case, I'm glad I didn't.

I wanted to build a pizza oven because I heard how awesome wood-fired pizza tastes from a brick oven. Our family has since found out we have many gluten and dairy allergies, but back when we could eat pizza, it was the most amazing pizza I had ever tasted. I asked my husband if he was willing to tackle a project that was kind of crazy. At that time, I heard about a man on the internet who was teaching courses to teach people how to build their own wood-fired oven.

This course was a *thousand dollars!* I still can't believe how people online can make a course on just about everything! Since we didn't have an extra thousand dollars lying around, we decided to do some research and figure out how to do the project ourselves. After all, if he could do it, so could we. We spent the spring researching and taking trips to the library. We included our kids in every step of the process as we drew plans for our pizza oven.

As soon as it was warm enough to start construction, we got to work. Our neighbor happened to be breaking up a concrete patio, and we asked him if we could use the remnants for the base of our brick oven. He was more than happy to share the concrete he was disposing of, so we excitedly built the base of our pizza oven together as a family. We had to communicate with our kids and figure out every part of the process. When parts were too difficult for the little kids, we had them watch and encourage.

By the time the actual *oven* part of our pizza oven was ready to build, we needed to find a good source for clay. We live right near the shores of a lake, so we asked around and found out that, of all things, a relative of my husband had a vein of pure clay running right outside his house in the lake bed. We *couldn't believe* it! We thought the clay was going to take a long time to find.

We took our kids over, scooped out massive amounts of clay, and hauled it back home in a trailer. Then came the most fun part of the project. We had a little kiddie pool we repurposed into our clay mixing station. We read about the correct amount of clay and sand to put into the mix to make it act like a brick. Then, we all took off our shoes and socks and stomped around in the clay mud until the mixture was the right consistency.

Next, we built the dome of the oven after carefully measuring and figuring out the math, a great time to put all of our hard work to practice! After constructing our oven, we let it dry and cure for a full two weeks. Finally, our pizza oven was ready to use. It was the talk of the town! We had people stopping by just to see it, and then, of course, they wanted samples of pizza. When we finally sold the house several years later, I must admit I was most sad to see our pizza oven go. That was a project we did together as a family, and we learned as we did it.

You might be wondering why we would make the effort to do such a crazy thing and why I'd be telling you. Wood-fired pizza is delicious, but was it really worth the hassle? Absolutely! We taught our kids that if you learn how to learn, you can do anything. Teach your kids that the sky's the limit, and they can learn how to do just about anything. Teach them to be self-learners. Don't let them rely on you for every academic question they have. Encourage them to figure some things out on their own. It will definitely build character.

If you teach your kids to become problem solvers, offering your guidance when needed, it will ease some of the responsibilities that you have. Handling your kids' academics is a huge responsibility. Add in the other hats you wear as a mom, and you have a lot on your plate. Remember to keep a balance.

Keep a Daily Schedule

For this reason, I can't stress enough the importance of a daily routine. A daily schedule will help you keep regular school hours. It's also helpful when people ask you to plan things during the homeschool day or stop by unexpectedly. I used to feel guilty for saying I couldn't do things because I was in the middle of homeschooling, but now, as I've established a daily routine, people have begun to understand and respect the fact that I'm tied up during the day, just like anyone else.

A daily routine will help you keep homeschool a priority. Your routine will look different than mine. Some people like to stick to a strict, rigid routine while others, like me, need something a little more flexible, but if you develop a basic framework for your day and fit in the major things you want to accomplish, it'll help you keep homeschooling a priority. Think of a schedule like a safeguard to keep you doing what you need to do. When you have a schedule and a plan, you'll be more likely to stick to your homeschool day.

My husband and I plan our homeschool year at the beginning of the year and try to stick to it as best as we can, making minor amendments as we go along. Just before the academic year gets started, we spend the night in a hotel away from the kids, planning and praying. We map out the school year, looking ahead to special occasions and holidays. Then, I print out an academic calendar, and we number the weeks so that, at a glance, I can have a basic idea of whether or not I'm on track.

This helps so much, and I highly recommend taking the time to do it. If, for some unforeseen reason, you get behind, you can tell pretty quickly how far off base you're. Unfortunately, I didn't always do this. Even though I thought I was staying pretty faithful, the kids and I were taking spontaneous days off throughout the school year. Eventually, those days off added up, and I suddenly found myself further behind than I thought.

Personally, I don't enjoy homeschooling during the summer, even though I know there are some families who do. My goal has always been to be done with school near the middle to end of May. At any given time, I know exactly where I'm in the school year because we have planned it out on the academic calendar. It's much easier to stick to a pre-arranged schedule when I can see it all laid out ahead of time.

The Best Ways to Keep Homeschool a Priority

Depending on where you're at in your homeschool journey, you may or may not struggle with keeping homeschool a priority. For me, it was especially difficult in the early years, when I was just starting to homeschool. It was a lot easier for me to skip a day of teaching, promising to make it up at some point. When I was only teaching a First and Third grader, there wasn't as big of a workload, so it was much easier to make up a day or two of school if I wanted to. Now that I'm currently teaching five kids, one in high school and two in junior high, I don't dare take an unnecessary day off. Actually, my kids don't like to take days off either because they know that while a day off is fun, they'll still have to get their work done eventually.

It's much better for you and your kids to have smaller amounts of schooling on a daily basis than to make up large chunks of school because you fell behind. It's much harder for your kids to learn that way, and it's also much less enjoyable to teach them.

In order to keep homeschool a priority, you can't over-schedule. There will always be more opportunities than time when you have kids. It seems like everywhere we go, there's something vying for our attention. I previously mentioned that we keep our kids' sports and extracurricular activities limited to a minimum. That's because homeschooling has to be one of our top priorities.

Remember our acronym BUSY? Busy means **B**eing **U**nder **S**atan's **Y**oke. If he can fill up every minute of your time, there won't be any time left for you to do the important things, and that may be all he needs in order to keep you from raising godly kids. I don't know about you, but I don't want to look back and remember my life was a harried mess, and I was too busy to teach my kids about the love of Christ.

Stay Faithful to the End

I've started a lot of things in my life. I have a craft room full of **UnFinished Objects**, or UFOs. There's something really fun about starting a new project. It's exciting to buy supplies, envision the finished product, and work at it until the first time I get stuck, and then I'm guilty of laying the project aside and leaving it there, never to be thought of again. Ashamedly, I've done this too many times to count. I want to make sure I don't do the same thing when it comes to teaching my kids. There's something about Monday morning, bright and early. It has the promise of new beginnings, and, just like my projects, it makes me excited, but do I have the same enthusiasm Friday afternoon? I want to stay faithful to the end, and I want to encourage you to stay faithful to the end as well.

There will always be the end of the day, the end of the week, the end of the year, and the end of the homeschooling career. I pray that God would make us faithful to finish strong in each of these time frames. Keep your head down and do the work. Stick to it and teach your kids there is reward in being faithful. I understand the temptation to taper off from school when more fun things come around, but, my friend, stay faithful. God will bless your efforts.

Sometimes, You Just Need a Break

There are some days that just warrant a mental health day. Even after I said not to blow off the school day, I want you to know it's okay to take a break sometimes. If we're doing really well, and school is running on track, then *occasionally*, without making it a habit, I'll declare a mental health day.

It's really fun to see the kids surprise as I announce that we're taking the day off of school, kind of like a snow day. I grew up in the Great White North, where we would get a foot of snow dumped on us overnight. I can remember waking up as a kid and listening intently to the radio broadcast to hear if my school was going to be canceled. It was so much fun and brought relief when the radio announcer declared a snow day. Obviously, snow days don't happen when you homeschool because you can do school regardless of what the weather is like, so, from time to time, give yourself and your kids a break and declare a spontaneous day off. You might even want to call it something fun like "pajama day" or something silly.

As I said, don't make it a habit, but recognize that everyone needs a break sometimes. We don't take breaks like the public school does, stopping for a teacher in-service day or various other random holidays, so, sometimes, we just need a fun day off. Go ahead! I'm giving you permission, just as long as you promise me not to make it a habit.

How to Stay Focused

Hopefully, just working through some of your priorities and deciding what's most important will help you weed out the unimportant things. That alone should help you stay focused on homeschool and make it a priority, but there are a few other things that might help as well. The first is to keep strong and clear boundaries with others. It's okay to let people know you homeschool and that you're not available to do certain things during the school day. I look at homeschooling as my job, and if I were working in an office, I wouldn't be available to help someone clean out their basement, for example. I also wouldn't be available to take a shopping trip or have a social lunch. You'll have to decide what your boundaries will be, but it's okay and even necessary to set them.

You also need to keep your distractions to a minimum. I find that I can actually be worse than the kids when it comes to distractions. All it takes is a quick peek at Facebook or my email, and I'm way off course. I can kid myself and think I'll just check my social media quickly and get right back to school, but we all know the rabbit trail that the internet leads to. Pretty soon, I'm stuck way off somewhere in cyberspace.

My recommendation? Keep your phone on airplane mode or tucked away somewhere far from where you're teaching. Don't feel like you have to answer every text, phone call, notification, ping, ding, buzz, whirl, or whatever other crazy sound your phone makes. It's okay to get back to people when you're free to give them the attention they're seeking.

Sick Days

Oh, sick days! I used to spend so much time trying to avoid any and all viruses. It didn't work, in case you're wondering, but I must admit I start to cringe as soon as flu season hits. Sick days can wreak havoc on a family that homeschools. There are nine people in our house; therefore, by the time a virus has run its course through each of us, I could be tending to sick people for a month or longer. Last year, I missed church for the entire month of February while tending to sick kids. You can imagine what happened with teaching.

It's inevitable. At some point, you and/or your kids *will* get sick, so, since you don't have any control over it, your only recourse is to embrace it. One of the joys of homeschooling is that you can still continue to get work done as long as your family isn't deathly ill. You can also make up the work and adjust the curriculum accordingly.

That's one of the reasons I'm very thankful that my kids aren't in school, so that we *can* adapt to sickness. When I was in second grade, I got the chicken pox, followed by the flu. I missed three weeks of school, and I remember the deficit when I got back. I missed a lot of education and teaching; thankfully, I had a teacher who was willing to help me make it up. When you homeschool, you can help your kids through the sick times and do a little bit of school work with them each day even though they're not feeling well. Just don't panic! You'll get back on track.

Bad Days

I wish I could tell you there will never be a bad day when you're homeschooling, but then you would know I was lying. The bad days will come; that I can promise, but a bad day, even a bad week, isn't a reason to stop homeschooling. You have to be firmly rooted in what you're doing and remember you're going to have bad days.

Keep an Eternal Perspective

One of the best things you can do for your kids is to invest in their eternity. Teaching your kids at home gives you the opportunity to impact their lives with the gospel. Your eternal investment has to be the main focus of why you homeschool. Think about how many hours you have each day to teach your kids about God and His love for them. You're impacting God's Kingdom right from your little homeschool classroom.

Your Why

Have you ever thought about your "why?" Have you ever been to a direct sales party? At some point during the presentation, the presenter will usually take a moment to tell you her "why." She'll usually say something about a goal she has in mind and how she hopes selling the product will get her to that point.

I did direct sales for a short amount of time, and one of the training assignments was to know my "why". What drove me to do what I was doing? And why did I want to do it? What did I hope to gain as a result? Let's just think about that for a minute. If direct sales companies want their employees to have a "why", shouldn't we also have our "why" as homeschooling moms?

Take some time to think about your "why". Ask yourself these questions:

- Why are you homeschooling your kids?
- Why are you making the sacrifice to do what you do?
- Why do you want to continue?
- Does what you're doing really matter?

Then, remind yourself it does matter. You're fulfilling The Great Commission right in your own home. That should make it easier to trust God's calling when you're tempted to throw in the towel. Your impact on your child, in your home right now, can mean all the difference in his eternity.

The Game Plan:

- Identify your fears. What makes you the most afraid regarding homeschooling your kids? List your fears and pray about them. Find verses in Scripture to help you combat your fears and then memorize them. Fight the fears with Scripture every time they threaten to make you afraid.
- Develop a plan to prepare for an unforeseen setback. Undoubtedly, you'll have days that don't go as planned. Make sure you know what to do by having it written down. Pare down your day to the basic things that absolutely *need* to be done. Write them down and go to that list when your day threatens to turn into a disaster.
- Plan a fun and personal day off for everyone. Make it special. Spend the day in your pajamas cuddling and relaxing. Play games if you would like to. Give yourself and your kids a day off, guilt-free.
- List the common struggles you face with homeschooling and then list the solutions. Keep the list handy so you can refer to it when you're tempted to become discouraged.
- Find your "why." Answer the questions mentioned at the end of the chapter to determine why you're homeschooling. Then, refer to your answers on a regular basis in order to stay focused.

Chapter 11
Balancing the Priority
Of Managing your
Finances

"There is no dignity quite so impressive and no independence quite so important as living within your means."
~ Calvin Coolidge

Homeschooling is expensive, and that reason alone may be enough to make you turn and shudder. *I've often* wondered why books cost so much, but when I consider the value of all the information in those books, I realize it's definitely worth it. If you've been homeschooling for any length of time, you know there's a financial sacrifice involved. In fact, making the choice to homeschool comes with many sacrifices for the entire family, but I believe it's a worthy choice. I'd much rather sacrifice monetary items and be able to teach my kids at home than to have all the riches the world has to offer and no influence over what my kids are learning.

Being a homeschooling mom will definitely limit your finances. Even if you're a mom who works and homeschools, (and if you are, my hat's off to you!) there will still be financial sacrifice. It's tempting to think that you can't afford to homeschool, but you must evaluate your priorities. Your finances need to be a priority as a homeschooling mom, but you also need to change the way you think about money and possessions. You'll definitely have to say no to things you could otherwise afford if you didn't need to purchase curriculum. Curriculum may very well be one of our family's major expenditures in any given year.

It's a Sacrifice

Homeschooling is a sacrifice for the whole family. Our kids go without a lot of things in order for us to afford the privilege of homeschooling. You see, it's not just the curriculum that's financially taxing; it's the fact that we're a single-income household because my time is dedicated to teaching the kids, but if you were to ask me, I'd tell you the eternal value is definitely worth it. I'm grateful to have the time to teach my kids God's Word and a love for Him.

You might have to let go of the idea of extravagant family vacations, but if you read Chapter Nine, you'll find many ways to spend time together as a family. You could also plan vacations that involve visiting family instead of staying in hotels or go camping instead of staying in a hotel. Get creative and find ways to spend time together that don't cost a lot of money. Here are a few more ways to save:

Don't eat out. I'm always amazed at how much it costs for our family to eat out at a "cheap" drive through restaurant. We can spend a lot of money even if we order from the value meal. Whenever possible, try hard to eat at home. Once in a while, if you can afford it, make sure to treat yourself and eat out as a special treat.

Plan out your groceries and menu. Work hard on your menu plan so you can eat the majority of your meals at home. You'll save a lot of money simply by being careful about your food. In Chapter Seven, we talked about menu planning and how with a little forethought, you can save money. You can shop sales, and if you stick to a menu plan and a list, you'll automatically save money because you won't be tempted to buy things that aren't on your list.

Stay home. I do really well with saving money if I'm at home, but if I go out of my house, I'm tempted to spend money every time I turn the corner, and it's usually on impulse items I *never* would have thought to buy otherwise. Going out equals spending money, so if you don't have to go out, stay home and save money.

Beware of your time online. There's so much propaganda on the internet, and everyone wants your money. I can't count how many times I've been surfing the web for recreation and suddenly seen something I wanted to buy that I didn't even know I couldn't live without. You used to have to go out of your house to impulse buy, but now, you can conveniently do it from your easy chair in the comfort of your own home.

Be careful if you do need to shop virtually. Have you ever noticed how Amazon is so nice and friendly and recommends other items you might want to purchase? Isn't that kind of them? Don't be fooled! Amazon doesn't care about you; they just want your money.

Unfortunately, when you shop online, there's less pain involved in punching a button versus handing someone cash. In other words, you don't really feel the financial strain when all you're doing is clicking "add to cart" or "buy it now". My suggestion is to shop from a list even when you're shopping online, just like you would in the store. And stick to that list!

Look for ways you can reduce your general living expenses. For example, I don't wear new clothes. It's rare for me to go shopping at a store that's not a thrift store, simply because I can't afford it. If you look carefully and take time, you can find some pretty nice things at thrift stores. I've heard the phrase, "Buy used and save the difference." That's an awesome idea, but we don't have the difference to save, so we simply don't buy new.

Evaluate your monthly expenses and see where you can cut. There's almost always something in your budget you can cut and live without. Cable is one of those things. With the internet having everything so readily available, you almost don't even need cable anymore. You can find many cheaper options online, but make sure you do allow yourself some money for entertainment, or it'll be easy for you to give up. Think about a diet. Have you ever restricted yourself from eating everything, only to find that at the first temptation, you wanted to eat something you shouldn't, and it ended in a binge session? The same is true with finances. If you keep your finances *too* tight, and never allow yourself *any* fun, you'll be much more tempted to binge at the first opportunity.

Organize Your Finances

In Chapter Seven, we talked about ways to organize, but we didn't touch on a budget. It's important to organize your money. Finances can be a huge source of stress and arguments. If you have a budget, it can really help the way your entire family runs. You need to be vigilant and watch so you know where your money goes. Since this isn't a book about finances, but rather about homeschool, I'm only going to discuss budget as it applies to homeschooling, but if you struggle with budgeting, I highly recommend you find a good course about budgeting and get your finances and budget under control.

Plan a monthly budget for curriculum and supplies. When my husband built our budget, we figured out how much our curriculum costs us on a yearly basis and divided that number by twelve. That's the amount of money we take out of his paycheck every month and specifically set aside for curriculum. We don't touch it other than to purchase our books and teaching material. We also have a small budget for school supplies that I use throughout the year. I find it much more helpful to have money specifically set aside for incidentals, so we're not trying to scrape money out of our general budget when I need more school supplies like ink cartridges or paper.

Make sure you don't dip into your homeschool budget for any reason. Honor your budget, and you'll be so happy you did. When the time comes to shop for curriculum, the money will be there waiting for you. I recommend sitting down with your husband and planning your budget together. Even if you're the one who runs the finances, it's good for him to be involved as well. Then, carefully and prayerfully consider your curriculum purchases just like you would any other purchase. Now, chances are, one of you is probably not as good with money as the other. That's okay, but I still recommend both of you be involved in setting up your budget. If the two of you have talked about your finances and planned it together, then you both should know your budget and its extent and will have a much easier time sticking to it.

Have a Plan for Your Curriculum

Next, you need to plan your curriculum. Don't wait until August to decide what you want to purchase. If you wait to purchase your curriculum, you'll be forced to buy under pressure, and, essentially, you'll end up spending more. Plan for the next year while you're currently teaching this year. That way, you can tweak things if necessary.

There are a few things to consider when buying curriculum, and, if you keep them in mind, it will be a breeze. In choosing your curriculum, you need to know ahead of time what you want for your homeschool classroom. I say "ahead of time" because if you wait to figure that out until you're shopping for the school year, you'll have a hard time choosing. There are so many quality options to choose from. It'll help you narrow it down if you have a basic idea of what you're looking for. In order to do that, there are a few questions you can ask yourself. Be sure to write down your answers. You'll want to refer to them as you shop around.

1. What are your goals and objectives for your students?

It's a good idea to have an end result in mind when you're homeschooling. Now, I realize that if your kids are little, this may be a bit hard to do, but it will help if you have a general idea.

- Do you want to make sure your students have a good handle on the arts?
- Are you concerned with state-level testing?
- Eventually, will you want your children to attend college?

These are just some questions to ask yourself so you can narrow the choices down more easily.

2. What's your style of teaching?

You'll want to choose a curriculum that fits your style. After all, if you don't like to teach it, it won't bring you or your kids much benefit.

- Do you enjoy reading aloud?
- Do you want to be hands-on in your approach to teaching or more hands-off?
- Do you want to have a school that's more literature-based or more science-based? Do you love history and want more of a historical emphasis?

- Do you want to use a classical approach?
- Do you prefer a traditional format?

3. What's your child's learning style?

In the same way your curriculum needs to match your teaching style, you'll want to make sure the curriculum you choose fits well with the style of learners you're teaching.

- Do your kids do well with visual learning?
- Are they strong readers?
- Is a hands-on approach better for your kids?
- Would an online curriculum suit them?

There's no right or wrong answer. You'll just want to answer these questions so you can have a better idea of the best curriculum for your kids.

4. What's your budget?

It's important to know how much money you have to spend on your curriculum because, if you don't know ahead of time, it's easy to overspend. Writing down the answers to these few simple questions ahead of time will help you when you choose.

- How much money can you commit to your homeschool classroom?
- Would you rather choose a free option?
- Does your school district have a program that helps homeschoolers?

5. Does the curriculum align with your family's values?

If you took the time to figure out your family's core values, choosing your curriculum is another great way to use them. If you haven't created core family values, I'd recommend taking the time to do so. In the meantime, consider:

- What translation of the Bible does your family use? Does the curriculum you're looking at use the same?
- What are your views of eschatology (the End Times) and does the curriculum line up with that?
- Are there any other important doctrinal issues you want your curriculum to include?

After answering these questions, you'll have a much better idea of what you're looking for. You won't be easily distracted by all the options, even though there are many good choices out there. Take the time to answer the questions prayerfully and carefully. Then, you'll be confident in your choice.

Stick to your Curriculum

Once you've chosen your curriculum, stick with it and give it your all! Obviously, nothing is perfect, and no curriculum will be one-hundred percent perfect, but keep tunnel vision and commit to teaching the curriculum you have so carefully chosen. After all, you put a lot of hard work into choosing it. It will help you save money by sticking to what you've already chosen.

Now, I love to research, and buying curriculum has become one of my all-time favorite hobbies. However, early on, I was guilty of always wanting bigger and better curricula, and I didn't do well with avoiding propaganda. Just when I thought I had everything set, I'd find something else that promised to make my child speak Latin by First Grade or read at a college level in elementary school. These claims are not true, by the way, but I bought into them - hook, line and sinker. Not only did I waste a lot of money, but it wasn't fun for the kids, either, because just when we'd start to settle into a curriculum, I wanted to switch. That got old fast. We all got tired of it. Now that I've committed to sticking with the curriculum I've chosen, I've saved a lot of money.

It'll always be tempting to wonder if your kids are getting what your neighbor's kids are getting at the public school, and as a result, you might be tempted to switch your curriculum. Don't do it! Avoid comparing yourself to others. I highly recommend you only change your curriculum if it's really not working for you or your kids, and only make that decision after giving it a really fair shake. Some kids will need different curriculum, and that's okay, but it's not the first thing you should do.

If you follow the plan I gave you, you'll know exactly what you're looking for, and it'll be much easier to avoid propaganda. Everyone claims to have the next *best* thing. Companies are interested in selling their product, and they want you to buy from them, so, naturally, they're going to tell you they have the *one* thing your child needs to be a success. However, when you think about it, math, reading, and science haven't really changed all that much over the years. You just need to teach your kids the basics. There will always be something new that you could try, but I'd like to encourage you to stick with what you bought and only change if it's really not working for you or your child. In the end, the best curriculum there is the one you actually use! You can spend hundreds of dollars on books that look amazing but only sit on your shelf. I know because I've done it.

Is it Reproducible?

Check your curriculum closely and know what you're buying. Many homeschool books can be reprinted if it's only used in your house. Oftentimes, companies will give you the rights to use the curriculum with multiple students. Consider if your curriculum is consumable or not. I've even found permission on the inside cover of many consumable products to reprint page if I use it strictly in my household. So check carefully to see if that's an option. You must consider whether or not it would be more economic to purchase another book versus the amount of money it would cost to copy it.

Stay Out of Debt

Please don't buy on credit. If you've set up a budget, you should have cash to buy your curriculum. Work as hard as you can to stay out of debt, even if it means going with a lesser option. It's best for you to stay within your means when buying your homeschool curriculum. My husband and I have also used our tax return for school curriculum. I know that not everyone receives a return, but if you do, consider this a great place to spend it.

What if I Really Can't Afford It?

There are many options available if you simply can't afford to purchase brand new curriculum. As always, I recommend you start by praying. Ask God for guidance and direction and that He would provide a way for you to homeschool.

Talk to other homeschoolers and ask if they have any curriculum you could borrow. Most homeschooling moms are more than willing to share curriculum with a fellow homeschooler who's just getting started or having trouble affording it. The first year I started homeschooling, I was gifted the entire year of curriculum. That set us off on the right foot and allowed us to save for the following year.

Check out your local homeschool co-op and participate in used curriculum swaps. These are usually pretty close to the end of the school-year and can be a great way to find curriculum you couldn't otherwise afford. Are you unsure where to find your local co-op? Type the name of your town and "Homeschool Co-op" in the search bar in Facebook. Sometimes, they're listed by the name of your county as well. Most homeschool cop-ops have a Facebook group and you should be able to find information within the group.

There are also many homeschool buying groups online and several options on Facebook. Just do a quick Google search to find out where. I'd suggest Googling the keywords "homeschool curriculum swap," or "used homeschool curriculum."

eBay is another great source for used homeschool curriculum. Watch for sales throughout the year. If you wait until August to purchase your curriculum, the market is extremely competitive, and you'll have a tough time winning items for a low price.

Check out sales of major homeschool curriculum companies. If you think about it, the majority of homeschoolers don't homeschool year-round, therefore, most homeschool companies aren't avidly selling their curriculum throughout the year. They're more likely to run sales in the middle of winter when no one is really looking for anything. If you've taken the time to plan ahead, you'll know exactly what you need. Then you can be ready to take advantage of any sales that come along.

Consider buying your curriculum a little bit at a time instead of in one large chunk. Again, this is another advantage to planning ahead. Keep a running list of the books and supplies you need and purchase them throughout the year. Your budget won't take as hard of a hit. It's much easier to buy one book at a time instead of thirty.

Check into charter schools. Charter schools are schools that pair up with your local school and have an allotment of funds that can sometimes be divvied up among homeschoolers. I haven't personally used one, as they're not available in my area, but I've heard of people using them and getting their curriculum and school supplies paid for by the grants. The best idea would be to check with your local public school superintendent. I was amazed to find out that sometimes Christians have been able to buy curriculum that's faith-based through the charter school grants.

Even if there aren't charter schools in your area, you can still check with your school district to see if they have any grants available for your kids. Many districts have options available they don't advertise.

There are also many free options to homeschool online. Again, do some research with good old-fashioned Google! Type in "free homeschool options" and see what comes up.

Don't forget to use your library. I've seen entire curriculum programs built around using your local library - all for free.

Recycle your Curriculum to Save Money

If you have more than one child, you can save an astonishing amount of money by recycling your curriculum. Of course, you'll need to hone your organizational skills, but if you get good at it, for the price of an organizational bin and a little bit of time, you can save yourself hundreds of dollars.

As soon as our school year is finished, I clean out our curriculum and organize it neatly into bins. I organize all my books according to grade level and store them appropriately. Then, I neatly label them so I know exactly what the contents are inside. That way, when the next child is ready to use them, they're all set and ready to go. Be faithful and diligent to preserve your curriculum. After all, it was probably a sacrifice for you to get it. As you well know, it costs money to buy curriculum, and you need to treat your curriculum as a valuable commodity.

I teach my kids to be easy on their books because they have siblings coming up behind them who'll need to use the book, as well. It's a great way to teach responsibility and a care and concern for others, so while I'm preserving my curriculum, I'm also teaching character training. Work hard to preserve your curriculum. You worked hard to get it; now make sure you get your money's worth out of it.

Don't Let Finances Be a Reason Not to Homeschool

Homeschooling is a sacrifice. There is cost involved, but it will be worth it in the end. With some careful planning and preparation, I believe that anyone who feels called to homeschool will be able to find a way.

The Game Plan:

- Identify areas you could conserve money in order to help with the expenses of homeschooling. Can you forgo coffee or a meal out to a restaurant? If you're already tight, think of one area you could conserve just a little bit more. Use the action points at the beginning of the chapter to help you from spending money unnecessarily.
- Plan a budget for your family, together with your husband. Find outside resources to help you. There are many useful resources online. Commit to honoring your budget by spending within your means.
- Use the questions listed to choose your homeschool curriculum. Take the time to commit to thinking through and answering each of the questions. When you've thoroughly evaluated, begin to shop for your curriculum, but only after you've finished.
- Work hard to stick to your curriculum as best as you can. Don't shop around after you have made your decision to purchase. Give your curriculum a fair shake before deciding it's not right for your family.
- Clean out your schoolroom (or area) as soon as school is finished and neatly store it away. Preserve your curriculum for the next set of kids who will use it.

Chapter 12
Balancing the Priority
Of Realizing it's All
About Surrender

"Let God have your life; He can do more with it than
you can."
~ Dwight L. Moody

By now, you know I consider motherhood a high calling. I believe motherhood is one of the most amazing privileges a woman can have. I'm unapologetically a stay-at-home wife and mom who enjoys homeschooling her children. I also believe motherhood is a ministry.

I know it can sometimes be hard to see motherhood as a ministry. There are some days when all you do is clean up messes, end squabbles, act as the maid, and try desperately to keep the house from burning down. If I'm honest, I like to think of ministry as a much nobler thing. Serving the poor in Africa, going to a distant land to teach the gospel, feeding the hungry children in India, ministering to an orphan...

Kids: The Ministry Right Before My Eyes

Why is it difficult for me to see my children as God's ministry right before my eyes? We know Jesus had a high view of children. In Matthew 19:14 (NIV), "Jesus said, 'Let the little children come to me, and don't hinder them, for the kingdom of heaven belongs to such as these.'" He was saying that even kids have a place, and we must not overlook them.

I wonder what would happen if I began to see motherhood as more of a ministry and less of a burden? Don't get me wrong; I love my children, and I'm sure you love yours, too, but does my attitude always reflect that? If I saw my kids as my ministry, would their interruptions seem more like blessings? Would I begin to feel privileged to sit up with a sick child in the middle of the night? Would mending a broken ankle or serving a sad child feel more like I'm serving God?

Colossians 3:23-24 (NIV) says, "Whatever you do, work at it with all your heart, as working for the Lord, not for human masters, since you know that you'll receive an inheritance from the Lord as a reward. It's the Lord Jesus Christ you're serving." *It's the Lord Jesus Christ you're serving*. Those words nailed me right between the eyes. They cut me straight to the heart. Being a homeschooling mom is hard work. Dare I even say it might be one of the most thankless jobs you'll ever do? But when I think about my job as a mom in light of what Scripture says, I can't help but see it differently.

My friend, right before you, in your very house, you have an opportunity to minister. Have you ever thought that, when you're serving your hungry child food, you're serving him in the name of Jesus? Has it ever occurred to you that as you serve that child food, you're being Christ's hands and feet, and it's as if you're serving Him directly? Consider the following passage:

> "For I was hungry and you gave me something to eat, I was thirsty and you gave me something to drink, I was a stranger and you

invited me in, I needed clothes and you clothed me, I was sick and you looked after me, I was in prison and you came to visit me.

Then the righteous will answer him, 'Lord, when did we see you hungry and feed you, or thirsty and give you something to drink? When did we see you a stranger and invite you in, or needing clothes and clothe you? When did we see you sick or in prison and go to visit you?'

The King will reply, 'Truly I tell you, whatever you did for one of the least of these brothers and sisters of mine, you did for me.'"
Matthew 25:35-40 (NIV).

Motherhood is a Privilege

If we begin to think of motherhood as a privilege, even a ministry, it changes everything. I wonder if, the next time we had to wipe a snotty nose, we remembered we were wiping it in the name of Jesus, would it make a difference? Would our attitudes be more loving? Why is it that I could go on a mission's trip to another far-off land and serve an orphan a plate of food, but when my child comes to me and asks what's for dinner, I bristle? If we start seeing children as a blessing and a privilege directly from God, will it begin to change the way we view parenting and motherhood?

The next time my child disobeys me, and I need to correct him, I can see it as an opportunity to advance the gospel. What a privilege, to have these little people right here before me all day long so I can teach them and direct them toward the Kingdom of God! Jesus gave his very life for me, and, in doing so, said that there is no greater love that anyone can have, than to lay down his life for a friend (John 15:13). That means when I lay down my life for my child, I'm walking in the footsteps of my Lord.

Sacrificially serving my children is *to be like Christ*. Then why is it so difficult? Why are there times I don't want to serve my children, that I'd rather be self-serving? When I began to see children as a ministry, my heart changed. Interruptions became opportunities to serve. Mistakes that my children made became moments to share the gospel.

We *all* need help. Sometimes, we miss the mark. Some days, I don't feel like I have shining mothering moments. Some days, I forget that I'm ministering here in my own home. Maybe it'll help to remember that your kids *will* fail. They're human and *will* make mistakes, and when that happens, don't shriek in despair; rather, embrace the opportunity to teach, to show love, to extend grace, to minister with the love of Christ. I want my motherhood to reflect Jesus. I want His love to be shown in my actions as I train and disciple my kids.

What's Your Calling?

So what exactly is your calling? If you truly do see motherhood as a ministry, what does that mean? Simply put, you're here to meet your kids' needs. Those needs start at birth and, from what I'm told, never actually end, though they do change. But your kids have an even greater need than clothes and food. They need to know Christ-crucified, and his love and grace, and you're the best possible person to teach them.

Don't for granted the time you have to spend with your kids as you homeschool and the opportunities that allows. Nurture their love for God throughout the homeschool day. They need you to give them biblical guidance. Your kids need you to show them love and grace, and they need you to connect that grace to God. Sometimes, you need to throw all the schooling and academics out the window and just love your kids. You're the one person they can count on. They need your direction. You might say your calling is: to teach your kids all about God and His saving grace.

Your Kids Need You

Your kids need your love, your time, your attention, and your acceptance. They need you to believe they're awesome, and they don't always need you to make them happy. Sometimes, your kids need your discipline. They need to know you care enough about them and love them enough to show them the error of their ways.

I often find myself telling my kids I care more about their holiness than their happiness. It's not my job as a mom to make sure my kids have everything they want and are never sad. I want to love them with the love of Christ and show them their need for a Savior. When you develop a relationship with your kids that runs deep, and they know you love and care about them because of the way you show it, you'll begin to see an awesome relationship develop between you and them. Your kids will want a close relationship with you. They'll want to be your friend. It takes time, but by loving your kids and serving them, *you'll show* them that you want their hearts.

Let them Know you Love Them

They need to know that no matter what, you'll always love them. Focus on your kids and make them one of your top priorities and ministry. My grandma told me a story about her sister-in-law who had seven kids. She said that no matter what, if one of the kids came into the kitchen where she was busy cooking, she always stopped, turned, and looked at her kids in the eyes and made them feel like she cared about what they were saying.

That takes sacrifice.

I must admit I'm guilty of doing exactly the opposite. Sometimes, I wonder how my kids must feel. I get so focused on what I'm doing that I forget I'm here to minister to my kids. I've been trying harder to make them feel like I care more about them than washing a sink full of dirty dishes. Make time for your kids. Make them feel special and like you care. Minister to your kids by making them a priority.

Motherhood is a Lifetime Commitment

You'll always be your children's mom. You won't always be their teacher. There will be a point where you have to let go and trust that the training you have given them will be enough. Remember the early years of parenting? Everything was new and exciting, and your child had to depend completely on you. There's a special joy in having a newborn baby in the house. You're extra careful and cautious with everything you do, sometimes even going overboard to meet every need as quickly as possible.

Then, your kids grew up a little bit, and you started homeschooling. You probably started out strong, but as time went on, you likely became less enthusiastic. Don't fade away over time. Keep up the enthusiasm you once had. Finish strong and remember you're in a lifetime commitment. Hopefully, you'll be encouraged to remember that when you serve your kids, you're directly serving God. You're ministering to Him in a way you may never have been able to if you never had kids.

Surrender to God

This ministry takes surrender. You don't exist on this earth to be your own person and serve your own needs anymore. Once you decided to have kids, you gave up that right, and, sometimes, surrendering oneself is a struggle. Jesus gave us the greatest example of surrendering our own wants and desires. He came to serve and not be served (Mark 10:45). The King of Glory gave Himself up for us in the most sacrificial way imaginable. This gives me the hope, faith, courage, and the desire to serve my kids and family in the same way. We can be examples to our kids if we follow Christ, the perfect example.

Have Christ's Attitude

How can you best serve your family? By having the same attitude in you that was also in Christ Jesus (Philippians 2:5-11). He's God Himself, yet He humbled Himself to die on the cross for us, the sinners of the world. Ask God to help you see your family as the greatest ministry you could ever serve here on this earth. Pray that you would learn to continually and daily give up your own desires for the sake of teaching your kids.

This should make all the difference in your attitude. It should make you want to be more Christ-like, more servant-like. "Whatever you do, work heartily, as for the Lord and not for men." (Colossians 3:23 ESV). If you have this perspective, it'll change the way you cook and clean. It'll change how you view sick kids and housework. It'll change the way you see your responsibilities as a homeschooling mother.

If you view everything you do in light of Christ's example, being a homeschooling mom will become a privilege and not a burden. Are you willing to die to yourself? Are you willing to surrender? Do you want to love God with your whole heart by serving your family first? God, in His grace, has given you an opportunity right before your very eyes to serve Him, right where you're.

It's true you won't have as much time to do the things you love. Your priorities will have to change. You may not ever become an expert crafter or have the career of your dreams, but in light of eternity, you're here making the biggest difference you ever could by being a homeschooling mom. Kids grow up fast. They really do. There are only so many hours in a day to influence them for the Kingdom of God. Pour all you can into your kids all day long. Teach them the ways of Scripture. Yes, being a homeschooling mom is a sacrifice, but it's also an awesome opportunity. The cost is high, but the payout is tremendous. In the end, what will you gain by teaching your kids at home? Remember, you can only bring people with you to heaven. You have been given the chance to teach your kids to love God and to live in eternity with Him forever.

I must continue to surrender my attitude to Christ. Daily, I need to seek Him and ask Him to change my heart, to keep me focused on

Him and the priorities that *He* has for me. When left to my own ways, I'd always choose to do what I most want to do. My priorities wouldn't be the way they are if it weren't for God's grace in my life. Homeschooling isn't easy. It's not easy to balance every priority, every responsibility, everything that's thrown at you as a homeschooling mom, but hard things are worthy things, and most things that are worthwhile are difficult to execute.

Homeschooling is really what you make of it. What's your attitude? Do you want to embrace this? Is doing the hard thing worth it to you? Do you see your kids as a ministry? Do you want to surrender your own desires? Do you want to say in the end that your time with your kids was worth it? You can become *Superwoman* and do anything you want to in the world, or you can devote your life to raising godly kids of integrity who will grow up to impact the world for Christ. That's your legacy of faith, and, in large part, it depends on your willingness to surrender and die to yourself.

Ask God to help you see raising kids and homeschooling as the highest calling you could have as a mother, to see it as a ministry and make it a top priority. I don't know about you, but to me, it's worth it!

What will you choose?

The Game Plan:

- Do you see homeschooling as an opportunity to minister to your kids? Ask God to help you appreciate the ministry before you. Pray that you'll have a sacrificial and loving attitude toward your kids.
- List the reasons you're grateful for being a homeschooling mom. Take time to reflect on them and develop an attitude of thankfulness for the privilege of teaching your kids.
- Look for ways to surrender your own wishes and desires for the greater purpose of teaching your kids.
- What legacy do you want to leave your kids? How are you achieving that?
- Do you see homeschooling your kids as a top priority? If not, begin to ask God to help you change your perspective. Search the Scriptures for encouragement to remind you that what you're doing is a noble thing – because it is!

Conclusion

My sweet friend, I've been homeschooling for twelve years. I've gone through periods of time where I've felt like I had no idea how I could handle it all. It's taken me to this point to realize that I can't.

Being a homeschooling mom means there are usually more obligations than enough of me to go around. I can't meet every need one-hundred percent of the time, and neither can you. I don't say this to discourage you but rather to let you know that balancing your life as a homeschooling mom is an ever-changing and constant process. It takes time and practice to juggle all you do.

I urge you please, to give yourself grace and remember that you'll never be able to handle it all. My intent in writing this book is to encourage you to find a balance between all your priorities. My hope is that you may lessen the load of guilt and the feelings of overwhelm. My prayer is that you'll take the actionable points I've included and begin to find joy as you juggle the priorities of your life. As you do so, you'll begin to feel like you have a better handle on the things that are important to you, and peace will reign in your life.

The priorities I've included in this book are not listed in any sequential order. They're things that, as a homeschooling mom, I've found need time, balance, and attention. You may choose to order them differently than I might. The key is to practice juggling each responsibility as you find contentment in being a homeschooling housewife. Much like a plate-spinning act, it's helpful to get a handle on one of your priorities, begin to feel like you're handling it well, and then add another responsibility.

Remember that the time you have with your kids truly is short. You won't be a homeschooling housewife forever, but while you're in this season, embrace the ministry God has given you. Your calling is important, and it doesn't go unnoticed. God sees your work, and He will bless you for it.

On the days you feel like you simply can't do it all - don't! Give yourself a break and start fresh tomorrow. You'll learn to juggle it all, one priority at a time.

Much love in Christ,
Amber

About the Author

Amber is a born again believer who lives out her faith by being a stay at home mom and wife. Since she was a little girl, she aspired to be a wife and a mommy. She happily homeschools five of her seven kids (two are still too little) and has been homeschooling for twelve years. She is the wife of a pastor. She and her husband Ben have made their home in the beautiful Upper Midwest. Her other writings can be found on allnaturaljoy.com and thehomeschoolinghousewife.org

Endnotes

[i] Lou Priolo, *The Heart of Anger* (New York: Calvary Press,1997), 61-64.

[ii] The idea of Circle time was first introduced to me on the blog, 'Preschoolers and Peace.com'

[iii] Kim Brenneman, *Large Family Logistics* (San Antonio: The Vision Forum, 2011), 133.

Made in the USA
Lexington, KY
14 February 2018